MW00568876

Brunch Life

MATT BASILE
AND
KYLA ZANARDI

BrunchLife

COMFORT CLASSICS AND MORE FOR
THE BEST MEAL OF THE DAY

PENGUIN

an imprint of Penguin Canada, a division of Penguin Random House Canada Limited

Canada • USA • UK • Ireland • Australia • New Zealand • India • South Africa • China

First published 2018

Copyright © Matt Basile and Kyla Zanardi, 2018

All rights reserved. Without limiting the rights under copyright reserved above, no part of this publication may be reproduced, stored in or introduced into a retrieval system, or transmitted in any form or by any means (electronic, mechanical, photocopying, recording or otherwise), without the prior written permission of both the copyright owner and the above publisher of this book.

www.penguinrandomhouse.ca

LIBRARY AND ARCHIVES CANADA CATALOGUING IN PUBLICATION

Basile, Matt, author
    Brunch life : comfort classics and more for the best meal of the day /
Matt Basile and Kyla Zanardi.

Issued in print and electronic formats.
ISBN 978-0-7352-3391-1 (softcover).—ISBN 978-0-7352-3392-8 (electronic)

    1. Brunches. 2. Cookbooks. I. Zanardi, Kyla, author II. Title.

TX733.B38 2018   641.5'2   C2017-907391-5
                                                 C2017-907392-3

Cover and interior design by Andrew Roberts
Cover and interior photography by Kyla Zanardi

Printed and bound in China

10 9 8 7 6 5 4 3 2 1

Penguin
Random House
PENGUIN CANADA

To our parents Mario, Rita, Lore, and Bernadette. Thank you for *always* believing in us. And to Ky's sister, Whitney, for liking me more even though we're not blood.

ALSO BY **MATT BASILE**

Street Food Diaries

Contents

INTRODUCTION

BREAKFAST IS A MEAL, BUT BRUNCH IS A CULTURE.

It's talked about, craved, and lined up around the block for. People will sit in bed and scroll through Instagram until a brunch picture so over-the-top egg-oozy, sugar-rush-inducing, and completely over-baconed pops up and has enough suggestive smell and taste powers to get them out of bed. Have you ever heard someone talk about their favourite brunch spot? It's almost a political debate—passion and conviction for all things covered in cheese, baked, then fried, and finally topped with a sunny-side-up egg. Brunch is something people get behind and believe in. It's habitual, it's comforting, and it has the power to let you indulge, allowing you to be you in the most liberating kind of way. You want to crush a bacon doughnut and two mimosas and wear track pants? Sure, why not! It's brunch, after all. So much more than just toast, or juice, or the godforsaken protein bar. It's happiness on a plate.

About seven years ago, before Ky and I started the Fidel Gastro's food truck or opened up Lisa Marie, I used to have this thing called a weekend. It was glorious, from what I remember. I rarely made plans ahead of time, but one thing was always set in stone: Sunday brunch. For the better part of a year, I would wake up every Sunday and walk on over to my local brunch spot in Toronto, The Stockyards. I would often go alone, sit at the bar, and order a cup of coffee, a basil lemonade, a bacon doughnut, and fried chicken and waffles. It was a two-hour window in my week that was reserved *for me*. I didn't have to say much to anyone. I could just shut out the world while I sat and ate. It didn't matter how long I waited or how long it took me to finish. It was about being immersed in my brunch life.

Monday to Friday I sat in a cubicle watching the sands of time fall very, very slowly. No matter what I had to deal with during the week, I knew that I had brunch to look forward to. It's practically all I talked about at work. We would have Monday morning status meetings and my turn would come. "Matt, what did you get up to this weekend?" The flurry of emotions this question unleashed. "Oh man oh man oh man, I had chicken and waffles for the first time ever. You mix hot sauce in the maple syrup and melted butter and you just cover it all and . . ." You get the idea. I took over the meeting with my brunch excitement, trying to get people to understand how much I loved brunch, trying to get them to share my excitement. I know this may seem pretty deep for a bacon doughnut, but it's true. Brunch became my way of understanding myself better, and then bringing people who were equally excited into that world.

When we opened our restaurant, Lisa Marie, we made sure to have a brunch that really captured my enthusiasm for this favourite meal. We wanted a menu that made people say, "What the fudge?" Five years later, we have a lineup every weekend, and I still get a rush from working the line in the kitchen. The only thing that makes me happier than waiting to eat this meal is watching a full restaurant of people eat our brunch.

Brunch Life brings together amazing brunch stories and recipes in one place. There are chapters completely devoted to eggs Benedict (pages 50–66) and chicken and waffles (pages 78–95). Whether you want to learn how to make OG Hollandaise (see page 50), how to jack up a dish with chimichurri sauce (see page 12), or how to whip up the crispiest fried chicken (page 76), it's all here. We have fun with all things bacon, indulge in a crap-ton of over-the-top pancakes (pages 126–146), and of course there's everyone's favourite brunch buddy, booze (pages 204–216). But brunch isn't just a blanket word for eating breakfast in the afternoon. It's a culture that's embraced differently everywhere you go. Throughout the book we've homed in on specific brunch cultures embraced by such cities as Toronto, Nashville, and San Francisco.

Page after page, *Brunch Life* aims to be just that—a showcase for everything and anything that makes brunch culture, a window into a food phenom that is all-consuming and radiant with fanfare. It's about the people who make it and the people who eat it. It's the eggs on your plate and the story of the chicken that made them possible as well as the rustic sourdough toast casually placed next to them and the story of the twelve-hour labour of love that went into baking it perfectly. It's being okay with waiting in line and finding hidden gems in your city. It's about snapping and filters and double tapping and tagging and all the other things cool kids do nowadays to let you know that brunch just happened. It's about being epic, being happy, doing it solo, or sharing that moment with others.

Brunch isn't just a meal—it's a way of life.

Brunch Classics

AT LISA MARIE, our brunch people come in for their staples, for that one thing that they've been craving all week. They're excited and happy to be a part of a club . . . dare I say, a breakfast club. The power of brunch is, in part, a result of its recurring, habitual nature. It involves traditions and go-to spots. I even have a pair of official brunch socks. But no matter what, it's the food that creates that initial attachment, the memories of where it all began. Like getting bacon and eggs after hockey practice. A stack of pancakes on the first day of summer. The smell of biscuits in the oven and the golden glow that would shine through the window. It's in these classics that memories were created. That being said, this chapter pays homage to brunch staples, like my Lamb Shank Hash (page 11). A hash is a diner staple, usually made with leftovers, but a lovingly braised lamb shank certainly fits the bill. The Family-Style Chimichurri Steak and Egg Tacos (page 12) include everything you love about traditional steak and eggs—including a beautiful piece of meat— but I love these because they're eaten with your hands (I'm still a kid at heart) and are shared. These are our brunch pioneers, our first loves.

SAUSAGE GRAVY AND BISCUITS

I think Ky and I ate biscuits in every single city we visited while researching for this book. Nashville biscuits were smaller, light, and fluffy little beauties served with jam and butter. Seattle had a much heartier version that was filled with so much gravy we almost couldn't tell they were even on the plate. San Fran's sat somewhere in the middle: super light and fluffy but way bigger than the ones in Nashville and filled with beautiful, beautiful meat. I have a few takes on biscuit batter throughout this book, but none more satisfying than this brunch icon.

SERVES 4

Biscuits
2½ cups (625 mL) all-purpose flour

1 tablespoon (15 mL) white sugar

1 tablespoon (15 mL) baking powder

1 teaspoon (5 mL) salt

5 tablespoons (75 mL) unsalted butter, frozen

1 cup (250 mL) 2% or whole milk

2 tablespoons (30 mL) Buffalo-style hot sauce

Sausage Gravy
1 pound (450 g) English breakfast sausages, removed from their casings

1 tablespoon (15 mL) unsalted butter

2 tablespoons (30 mL) all-purpose flour

¼ cup (60 mL) sparkling white wine

½ teaspoon (2 mL) chili flakes

1 teaspoon (5 mL) salt

2 cups (500 mL) 2% milk

For Serving
2 tablespoons (30 mL) canola oil

4 large eggs

8 slices American cheddar cheese

¼ teaspoon (1 mL) roughly chopped fresh sage, for garnish

MAKING A BISCUIT, BABY
Preheat the oven to 425°F (220°C) and line a baking sheet with parchment paper. In a large bowl whisk together the flour, sugar, baking powder, and salt. Use the large holes of a cheese grater to grate the frozen butter into the dry ingredients. Crumble the grated butter and flour together with your fingers until the mixture resembles pea-size crumbles. Add the milk and hot sauce and mix everything together with your hands until it just forms a dough. On a lightly floured surface, roll out the dough until it is approximately 1 inch (2.5 cm) thick. Use a 2-inch (5 cm) round cookie cutter to cut 4 or 5 biscuits out of the dough. Place biscuits on the prepared baking sheet, leaving an inch or two between them. Bake for about 12 minutes, until golden brown. Transfer biscuits to a rack and allow them to cool to room temperature.

RELEASE THE MEAT!
Heat a large saucepan over medium-high heat, then add the sausage meat. Break the sausage into small chunks with the back of a wooden spoon and cook, stirring frequently, for 4 to 5 minutes, or until it is cooked through and starting to brown. Use a slotted spoon to remove the meat from the pan and set it aside in a bowl. Melt the butter in the pan, then add the flour, stirring with a wooden spoon to form a thick paste. Add the sparkling wine, chili flakes, and salt and whisk to incorporate. Turn the heat down to medium-low and slowly add the milk while whisking constantly, until it starts to thicken. Return the cooked sausage and turn the heat back up to medium-high. Continue stirring constantly as the gravy thickens, about 5 minutes. Remove from the heat and keep warm.

In a medium frying pan, heat the canola oil over medium-high heat. Crack the eggs into the pan and turn the heat down to medium. Cook the eggs sunny side up for about 5 minutes.

THAT'S BISCUIT, BABY
To serve, slice the biscuits in half and top each half with a slice of cheddar. Ladle the Sausage Gravy over the cheesy biscuits and top each serving with a sunny-side-up egg. Garnish with chopped sage.

LAMB SHANK HASH

Hash is awesome. It's the perfect refrigerator clean-out meal—a great opportunity to make a delicious brunch using whatever you have in your fridge. Really, the only things that make hash a hash are the carrots, potatoes, and other hearty veg. Then all you need is a protein and a sauce to bring it all together. This recipe uses a lamb shank, because that's what I had left over in the fridge one day. See how resourceful hash can be? I want you to try reinventing your own leftovers one morning. Leftover ribs from the grill? Great . . . barbecue rib hash. Leftover turkey and gravy from Thanksgiving? Beauty . . . turkey hash. See what I mean?

SERVES 4

SHANK YOU KINDLY

Heat the canola oil over medium-high heat in a medium, heavy pot or Dutch oven. Place the lamb shanks in the pot and sear for 2 minutes on each side. Remove the lamb from the pot and set aside. Add the carrot, celery, and onion to the pot and sauté for 2 minutes, stirring constantly. Add the lemon juice, soy sauce, Worcestershire sauce, sage, thyme, rosemary, mustard, onion powder, salt, pepper, and chili flakes. Stir to incorporate. Return the lamb shanks to the pot and add the water. Turn the heat down to medium-low, cover, and leave to braise for 2 hours, or until the meat is very tender. Turn off the heat, transfer the lamb shanks to a plate, and allow them to sit for 15 minutes. Then, using two forks, pull all the meat from the bones and shred it into medium chunks. Discard the bones and stir the lamb meat back into the gravy in the pot. Cover and keep warm.

HOT POTATO COMING THROUGH

Place the potatoes in a medium saucepan and cover with water. Bring to a boil and cook until fork-tender, about 10 minutes, then drain. Melt the butter in a large frying pan over medium-high heat. Add the potatoes and fry until crispy all over. Add them to the Braised Lamb.

In a medium frying pan, heat the canola oil over medium-high heat. Crack the eggs into the pan and turn the heat down to medium. Cook the eggs sunny side up for about 5 minutes.

Serve the Lamb Shank Hash on a large platter with sunny-side-up eggs on top.

Braised Lamb

1 tablespoon (15 mL) canola oil
2 lamb shanks (about 1 pound/450 g each)
1 cup (250 mL) roughly chopped carrots
1 cup (250 mL) roughly chopped celery
1 cup (250 mL) roughly chopped Spanish onion
Juice of 1 lemon
2 tablespoons (30 mL) soy sauce
1 tablespoon (15 mL) Worcestershire sauce
1 tablespoon (15 mL) finely chopped fresh sage
1 tablespoon (15 mL) finely chopped fresh thyme
1 tablespoon (15 mL) finely chopped fresh rosemary
2 teaspoons (10 mL) Dijon mustard
1 teaspoon (5 mL) onion powder
1 teaspoon (5 mL) salt
½ teaspoon (2 mL) black pepper
½ teaspoon (2 mL) chili flakes
4 cups (1 L) water
5 red potatoes, cubed
4 tablespoons (60 mL) unsalted butter

For Serving

2 tablespoons (30 mL) canola oil
4 large eggs

FAMILY-STYLE CHIMICHURRI STEAK AND EGG TACOS

The first time I saw steak and eggs on a menu, I was convinced it was a mistake. I honestly thought the diner meant "bacon" instead of "steak." Sure enough, I was wrong. My love for steak is as strong as my love for sunny-side-up eggs, and in that moment, my worlds collided. As much as I love this classic dish, I've also been burned by many badly cooked steaks. Without a proper thick-cut, well-marbled steak, this dish just shouldn't exist. This version really does focus on the steak part. Yes, the eggs matter, but for this dish to shine, you're going to have to make friends with a butcher.

───────────────── SERVES 4 ─────────────────

Steak
1 bone-in rib steak (2 pounds/900 g and
    about 2½ inches/6 cm thick)
1 tablespoon (15 mL) canola oil, plus
    more for rubbing steak
1 teaspoon (5 mL) salt
1 teaspoon (5 mL) black pepper

Grilled Onions
1 red onion
1 white onion
1 tablespoon (15 mL) canola oil

Chimichurri Sauce
6 cloves garlic, peeled
1 cup (250 mL) cilantro leaves
Juice of 2 limes
½ cup (125 mL) extra-virgin olive oil
1 teaspoon (5 mL) salt

For Serving
6 large eggs
1 tablespoon (15 mL) unsalted butter
8 corn tortillas

NOW THIS IS A STEAK!
Preheat the oven to 350°F (180°C). Allow the steak to rest at room temperature for 15 minutes. Rub both sides of the steak with a little bit of canola oil, then season with salt and pepper. Heat a large cast-iron frying pan over high heat. Pour 1 tablespoon (15 mL) of canola oil on a piece of paper towel and wipe the pan. Add the steak to the pan and sear for 3 minutes on each side. Be sure to stand the steak on its side and render the fat for 2 to 3 minutes. Lay the steak down in the pan, transfer the pan to the oven, and cook for 12 minutes for a medium-rare steak, 15 minutes for medium, or 18 minutes for medium-well. Remove the steak from the oven, transfer it to a cutting board, and set aside to allow it to rest.

NOW FOR ALL THE FIXINGS
Slice the red and white onions ½ inch (1 cm) thick and separate the slices into rings. Heat the canola oil in a medium grill pan over medium-high heat. Add the onions and cook for 5 to 6 minutes, or until they begin to soften. Remove from the pan while they still have a little firmness and are not too soggy.

To make the Chimichurri Sauce, place the garlic, cilantro, lime juice, olive oil, and salt in a food processor and blend for 1 to 2 minutes, until the garlic and cilantro are fully processed.

Crack the eggs into a bowl and whisk until smooth. Melt the butter in a large non-stick frying pan over medium heat. Pour the eggs into the pan and cook, stirring frequently, until cooked through but still soft and moist, about 8 minutes. Use a wooden spoon or rubber spatula to remove the scrambled eggs from the pan. In the same pan over medium-high heat, lightly toast the tortillas.

Slice the steak off the bone, then thinly slice the meat against the grain. Serve family style by fanning steak slices on a large plate beside the bone. Drizzle some Chimichurri Sauce over the steak. Arrange the scrambled eggs, Grilled Onions, and tortillas on a platter and serve the rest of the Chimichurri Sauce on the side.

PORK BELLY AND EGGS WITH CREAMED CORN

There's no dish that's more representative of breakfast or brunch than bacon and eggs. I know for a fact that the smell of bacon cooking has gotten me out of bed. And as awesome as bacon is, the eggs have always been my favourite. Two of them, cooked sunny side up, with a side of buttered bread to dip. Oh man. Now that's heaven. There are so many ways you can make this dish, and in this recipe I'm using pork belly and creamed corn. You might be thinking, Matt, I like bacon, but what's this pork belly you speak of? Well, good news, folks, bacon *is* pork belly, just cured. So you're still getting your bacon, just in a different package. And then there's the creamed corn, so velvety and sweet. It works nicely with the meaty pork belly.

SERVES 4

ROAST THAT BELLY GOOD
Preheat the oven to 325°F (160°C). In a small bowl stir together the canola oil, honey, paprika, and salt. Rub the mixture onto all sides of the pork belly. Place the pork belly on a rack nestled into a baking sheet and roast for 3 hours, or until it is a gorgeous dark colour (not to be confused with burnt!). Remove the pork belly from the oven and allow it to rest for 5 minutes. Cut the meat against the grain into ½-inch (1 cm) slices and set aside.

NOW TO CREAM SOME CORN
Bring a large pot of water to a boil. Add the corn cobs and boil for 8 minutes. Remove the corn from the water and allow it to cool. Slice the kernels off the cobs. Transfer the kernels to a food processor and add the mozzarella, cream, and salt. Pulse just until most of the corn is blended in—you want some of the corn to stay whole, which will add a nice texture to the Creamed Corn. Set aside.

In a large frying pan, heat the canola oil over medium-high heat. Crack the eggs into the pan and turn the heat down to medium. Cook the eggs sunny side up for about 5 minutes. Repeat until all eggs are cooked, if necessary.

HAPPY PLATE, HAPPY DATE
While the eggs are cooking, toast the bread. Heat a large grill pan over high heat and lightly grill your pork belly slices to heat them up. Fill each plate with 3 slices of pork belly, 3 sunny-side-up eggs, and a scoop of Creamed Corn. Sprinkle a little paprika over the corn. Serve with toast.

Pork Belly
½ cup (125 mL) canola oil
¼ cup (60 mL) honey
2 teaspoons (10 mL) smoked paprika
2 teaspoons (10 mL) salt
1 boneless, skinless pork belly
    (2 pounds/900 g)

Creamed Corn
4 corn cobs
¼ cup (60 mL) finely shredded
    mozzarella cheese
2 tablespoons (30 mL) heavy (35%)
    cream
1 teaspoon (5 mL) salt
½ teaspoon (2 mL) smoked paprika

For Serving
3 tablespoons (45 mL) canola oil
12 large eggs
8 slices bread, preferably white

MASCARPONE SOFT SCRAMBLE

I don't talk about it much, but truth be told, I worked the breakfast shift at my university campus bar. It was easy work. I'd get up at six, go in and prep everyone's station, cook eggs for three hours, then go to class (and at the end of the day, drink beer!). Easy peasy. But have you ever seen how scrambled eggs are cooked in a place like that? It's a sin. Hot oil in a pan, burner turned all the way up, and two whisked eggs quickly cooked while being stirred around a bit. It always made me sad. Proper soft scrambled eggs need time, low heat, and slow mixing. And on top of that, some fat—butter and cheese—makes them more luscious.

═══════════════ SERVES 4 ═══════════════

1 cup (250 mL) fresh or thawed frozen
　　green peas
½ cup (125 mL) freshly grated Parmesan
　　cheese
¼ cup (60 mL) + ⅓ cup (75 mL)
　　mascarpone cheese
10 large eggs
1 tablespoon (15 mL) unsalted butter
Salt and black pepper

GREEN EGGS, HOLD THE HAM
Place the green peas, Parmesan, and ¼ cup (60 mL) mascarpone in a food processor and pulse until most of the peas are broken down and the cheese is incorporated.

ADD THAT ITALIAN FAT
Crack the eggs into a large bowl and whisk in the remaining ⅓ cup (75 mL) mascarpone. Melt the butter in a large non-stick frying pan over medium heat. Pour the egg mixture into the pan and cook slowly, pushing the eggs around the pan with a rubber spatula. When the eggs are three-quarters cooked, after about 6 minutes, add dollops of the pea and mascarpone mixture. Continue to cook gently and stir, allowing the cheese to melt.

To serve, transfer the Mascarpone Soft Scramble to a serving plate and season with salt and pepper.

HUEVOS RANCHEROS

Brunch is all about satisfying a craving. You look at a menu and ask yourself, Which dish completes me? Is it something for your sweet tooth? A deep-fried option? Spice? Or even something as simple as a few runny eggs? Sometimes you get a dish that checks off several boxes, and for me that's always huevos rancheros. My version is hearty and saucy, and it's got spice *and* runny eggs. If you want to cool it down a bit, add more sour cream and queso fresco, or use only half of the green chili pepper. You can serve it vegetarian, like I do here, or feel free to add whatever toppings you see fit, like seafood (mmmm, shrimp), more guacamole, extra jalapeños, refried black beans, hard chips, or salsa verde.

SERVES 4

SALSA GONE ALL RANCHERO
Heat the canola oil in a medium saucepan over medium-high heat. Add the shallots and garlic and sauté for 2 minutes, or until they become translucent. Add the red pepper and green chili pepper and continue sautéing for another 3 minutes. Add the water, tomatoes, chili powder, salt, and black pepper; stir to combine. Turn the heat down to medium, add 1 teaspoon (5 mL) butter, and cook for 10 minutes, stirring occasionally. Turn the heat down to low, add the black beans and the remaining 1 teaspoon (5 mL) butter, stir thoroughly, then remove from the heat and keep warm.

AND NOW WE HUEVOS
In a medium frying pan, heat the canola oil over medium-high heat. Crack the eggs into the pan and turn the heat down to medium. Cook the eggs sunny side up for about 5 minutes. At the same time, heat a large frying pan over high heat and lightly toast the tortillas on both sides.

NOW MAKE THOSE SIMPLE EGGS DANCE
To assemble, arrange the tortillas on plates and top each with 1 sunny-side-up egg. Spoon the Salsa around the eggs and over the tortilla. Garnish with crumbled queso fresco, cilantro, and a drizzle of sour cream.

Salsa
1 tablespoon (15 mL) canola oil

3 shallots, roughly chopped

2 cloves garlic, roughly chopped

1 sweet red pepper, cut into ¼-inch (5 mm) slices

1 large green chili pepper, diced (use half if you do not like spice)

½ cup (125 mL) water

4 Roma tomatoes, chopped

1 tablespoon (15 mL) chipotle chili powder

1 teaspoon (5 mL) salt

¼ teaspoon (1 mL) black pepper

2 teaspoons (10 mL) unsalted butter, divided

1 cup (250 mL) canned black beans, drained and rinsed

For Serving
2 tablespoons (30 mL) canola oil

4 large eggs

4 small (6-inch/15 cm) corn tortillas

3 tablespoons (45 mL) crumbled queso fresco (or any soft fresh cheese)

¼ cup (60 mL) chopped cilantro

2 teaspoons (10 mL) sour cream (double this if you do not like spice)

LOBSTER AND SCRAMBLED EGG DIM SUM

When Ky and I were vacationing in Cape Cod a few years back, the seafood we ate was next level. It's so fresh and abundant. A few days into the trip, we both noticed that restaurant menus were all pretty much the same: whole lobster, lobster roll, shrimp cocktail, and clam chowder. I'm not complaining, but once in a while you'd like to eat something different with these beautiful ingredients. Luckily, we popped into a little takeout spot and had the most amazing lobster dumplings ever. Back home, we added a few extra flavour components, including the sweet and spicy dipping sauce and a sour, crunchy salad to serve with the dumplings. Before you start this dish, you might want to enlist the help of someone who has small fingers. Trust us, dumplings require quite a bit of finger work.

SERVES 4

Sesame Salad

1 cucumber, sliced ¼ inch (5 mm) thick
½ cup (125 mL) thinly sliced red onion
1 tablespoon (15 mL) salt
2 tablespoons (30 mL) cilantro leaves
1 teaspoon (5 mL) sesame seeds
1 teaspoon (5 mL) rice wine vinegar
½ teaspoon (2 mL) sesame oil

Sweet and Spicy Dipping Sauce

1 tablespoon (15 mL) hoisin sauce
1 teaspoon (5 mL) soy sauce
1 teaspoon (5 mL) Sriracha hot sauce
Juice of ½ lime

Lobster and Scrambled Egg Dumplings

10 ounces (280 g) cooked lobster meat,
    pulled apart
2 Thai red chili peppers, sliced
¼ cup (60 mL) sliced green onion
½ teaspoon (2 mL) cornstarch
½ teaspoon (2 mL) salt
½ teaspoon (2 mL) sesame oil
Grated zest of 1 lime
3 large eggs, divided
25 wonton wrappers
5 teaspoons (25 mL) canola oil, divided
1 cup (250 mL) water, divided

SALAD ON THE SIDE

Place the cucumber and red onion in a colander and sprinkle with the salt. Toss well and set aside in the sink or over a bowl for 15 minutes. This will help draw the moisture from your vegetables and give a slightly pickled quality to the salad. Gently press the cucumber and red onion between paper towels to extract as much liquid from them as possible. Place in a medium bowl and add the cilantro, sesame seeds, vinegar, and sesame oil. Toss well and set aside.

In a small bowl stir together the hoisin, soy sauce, Sriracha, and lime juice. Set the Sweet and Spicy Dipping Sauce aside.

I'VE GOT A FILLING . . .

In a medium bowl combine the lobster meat, chili pepper, green onion, cornstarch, salt, sesame oil, lime zest, and 2 eggs. Mix thoroughly with your hands. Line a baking sheet with parchment paper.

Lightly whisk the remaining egg and set aside. Place 1 teaspoon (5 mL) lobster mixture in the centre of a wonton wrapper. (Keep the remaining wrappers covered in plastic wrap.) Moisten your finger with the whisked egg and run it along all four edges of the wrapper. Fold the wrapper in half to create a triangle and press firmly along the edges to seal. Working from one end of the triangle to the other, pleat the wrapper every ¼ inch (5 mm) or so to create an accordion pattern. Place the sealed dumpling on the prepared baking sheet and finish making all 25 dumplings. Heat 1 teaspoon (5 mL) canola oil in a non-stick frying pan over medium-high heat. Place 5 dumplings in the pan and fry for 30 seconds. Pour 2 tablespoons (30 mL) water into the pan, quickly cover with a lid, and allow the dumplings to steam for 2 to 3 minutes, until the egg on the inside is fully cooked and the wrappers are more opaque. Transfer the dumplings to a medium bowl lined with paper towel. Repeat this process until all the dumplings have been fried and steamed.

Serve the Lobster and Scrambled Egg Dumplings family style with the Sesame Salad and Sweet and Spicy Dipping Sauce on the side.

Anatomy of an Egg

The glorious sunny side up. Part white, part yolk . . . all awesomeness

THE YOLK
The best part, according to my grandfather. Perfect for dipping bread. Please don't overcook it.

INNER WHITE
Acts like a pillow for the yummy yolk. Contains a lot of protein.

OUTER WHITE
The part that gets nice and crispy, and usually gets scarfed up first.

Brunch in Buns

NICE BUNS. HEY, it's the truth. A sandwich is only as good as the bread that holds it together. You can take anything you want, slap an egg on it, and call it brunch, but the question remains, Will the buns hold up? So often Ky and I have been out for brunch and we've been so incredibly excited about an epic sandwich only to have it ruined by a flawed bun. The elements that go inside are, of course, equally important. Are they balanced? Is there a good ratio of meat, toppings, and runny yolk? Is the sandwich innovative or a classic? Can you dip it? Crush it? Cut it in half? All very thought-provoking questions. (Well, not really, except for the purposes of this book.) But what does make the perfect brunch sandwich? This chapter looks at all sorts. Most contain bacon, like The Great Canadian Breakfast Sandwich (page 31). All have an egg or two, and as at most delis, cheese and pickles are always optional. No matter what tickles your fancy, let it be known that something delicious in a bun is an integral part of brunch.

WESTERN OMELETTE GRILLED CHEESE

As a kid who grew up playing hockey, I was always going to out-of-town tournaments with my dad. There were lots of team meals, but my dad and I would make a point to separate from the group for breakfast. My dad has always been drawn to greasy spoons, so we naturally gravitated to these small diners to chow down. I'm not sure what attracted him the most—the humbleness of the surroundings, the honesty of the food, or the fact that the lady cooking bacon in the back owned the place and employed all her grandkids—but his greasy-spoon go-to was always a western omelette. This one's for you, Dad.

SERVES 2

Western Omelette

1 tablespoon (15 mL) canola oil

¼ cup (60 mL) diced button mushrooms

¼ cup (60 mL) diced yellow onion

¼ cup (60 mL) diced sweet red pepper

2 ounces (55 g) pancetta, diced

½ teaspoon (2 mL) chili flakes

¼ teaspoon (1 mL) salt

4 large eggs

1 teaspoon (5 mL) Sriracha hot sauce

For Serving

4 slices light rye bread

1 tablespoon (15 mL) unsalted butter

4 slices Havarti cheese

WELCOME TO THE RANCH

In a medium frying pan, heat the canola oil over medium-high heat. Add the mushrooms, onion, red pepper, pancetta, chili flakes, and salt. Sauté for 6 minutes. Meanwhile, crack the eggs into a bowl and whisk until smooth. Add the Sriracha and whisk to incorporate. Pour the spicy egg mixture into the pan of veggies, turn the heat down to medium-low, and cover the pan. Cook the eggs, undisturbed, for 5 minutes. Carefully flip the omelette and cook, uncovered, for an additional 2 minutes. Remove the omelette from the pan and cut it in quarters.

YEEHAW!

While the omelette is cooking, toast the rye bread. Heat a large frying pan over medium-high heat. Spread the butter on one side of all 4 pieces of toast. When the pan is hot, add the bread, buttered side down, and lay a slice of Havarti on each slice of bread. Turn the heat down to medium and fry until the bread is crispy and the cheese melts.

To assemble, place two western omelette quarters between two pieces of cheesy toast.

THE GREAT CANADIAN BREAKFAST SANDWICH

Oh, Canada. Home to hockey, flannel/denim combinations, and peameal bacon, also known as Canadian bacon. Widely considered the most Canadian thing you can eat, peameal is cured and salted pork loin covered in cornmeal (historically it was chickpea meal, hence the name). If you ever find yourself at a Canadian carnival, fair, or farmers' market that doesn't offer up these sandwiches, then leave, they're phonies. My theory on the bacon sandwich is, if you're going to make it, make it as Canadian as possible. This version ensures that yes, you might wear half of it, but also yes, you will be in love.

=== SERVES 2 ===

ONIONS, EH?

Heat a large frying pan over medium-high heat and melt the butter. Add the sliced onions and cook, stirring frequently, until translucent. Season the onions with salt and continue cooking for another 7 minutes. Turn the heat down to medium-low and add the cinnamon and maple syrup. Stirring occasionally, cook the onions for 15 minutes. Remove the onions from the pan and set aside.

BACK BACON A.K.A. PEAMEAL BACON A.K.A. CANADIAN BACON

Using the same frying pan, turn the heat back up to medium-high and fry the strip bacon for 2 minutes on each side, or until crispy. Remove the bacon from the pan and set it aside to drain on a plate lined with paper towel.

Again using the same pan (and the bacon grease!), turn the heat down to medium and cook the peameal bacon on the first side for 2 minutes. Flip the bacon and cook for another 5 minutes. In the pan, arrange the peameal bacon into 2 stacks of 3 and lay 2 slices of cheddar on top of each stack. Cover the pan and leave on the heat for 1 to 2 minutes to allow the cheese to melt.

While the cheese is melting over the bacon, heat the canola oil in a small frying pan over medium-high heat. Crack the eggs into the pan and turn the heat down to medium. Cook the eggs sunny side up for about 5 minutes.

IF YOU BUILD IT, THEY WILL EAT

To assemble, place 3 slices of strip bacon on the bottom half of each brioche bun. Layer each with a peameal and cheese stack, and top with a healthy spoonful of Maple Syrup Onions. Finish each sandwich with a sunny-side-up egg and the top of the brioche bun.

Maple Syrup Onions

1 tablespoon (15 mL) unsalted butter
4 small yellow onions, thinly sliced
1 teaspoon (5 mL) salt
2 teaspoons (10 mL) cinnamon
¼ cup (60 mL) real Canadian maple syrup

For Serving

6 strips bacon
6 slices Canadian (peameal) bacon
4 slices orange cheddar cheese
1 tablespoon (15 mL) canola oil
2 large eggs
2 brioche buns, sliced in half

CROQUE SURPRISE

Our cooking style has never been deeply rooted in French cuisine. That said, we have nothing but respect for it. After all, its ingredients lend themselves well to brunch. Cheese, charcuterie, bread, butter, cream—you get the idea. One could argue about which French brunch staple is better, the croque monsieur or the croque madame. But good news, folks—this one beats them both.

SERVES 2

Béchamel Sauce

3 tablespoons (45 mL) unsalted butter

1 tablespoon (15 mL) finely chopped fresh sage

3 tablespoons (45 mL) all-purpose flour

1½ cups (375 mL) 2% or whole milk

1½ cups (375 mL) finely grated Parmesan cheese

Croque Surprise

4 slices egg bread, such as challah

1 tablespoon (15 mL) Dijon mustard

4 slices cooked Italian-style ham

½ cup (125 mL) shredded mozzarella cheese, divided

1 tablespoon (15 mL) unsalted butter

2 large eggs

For Garnish

Dijon mustard

Baby cornichons

BÉCHAMEL SAUCE—FRENCH FOR "REALLY AWESOME, CALORIE COUNT DOESN'T MATTER" SAUCE

In a medium saucepan, melt the butter over medium heat. Sprinkle the sage and flour over the melted butter and whisk for about 1 minute, until a paste forms. Turn the heat up to medium-high and slowly pour in the milk while constantly whisking. Continue to cook, whisking, as the sauce thickens. Turn the heat back down to medium, add the Parmesan, and whisk until melted. Remove from the heat.

QUELLE SURPRISE! IT'S LIKE A TOAD-IN-A-HOLE

Preheat the oven to 400°F (200°C). Lay the bread on a cutting board and spread a thin layer of mustard over each slice. Lay 1 slice of ham on each piece of bread. Sprinkle ¼ cup (60 mL) mozzarella on each of 2 slices of bread. Close the sandwiches, then use a 2-inch (5 cm) round cookie cutter or a glass to cut out the centre of each sandwich. Do not discard the mini centre sandwiches.

TWO SANDWICHES FOR THE PRICE OF ONE

In an ovenproof frying pan, melt the butter over medium-high heat. Fry sandwiches (and the mini sandwiches!) for 1 minute, or until golden brown and crispy. Flip the sandwiches. Crack an egg into the hole of each large sandwich. Place the whole pan in the oven and bake for 12 to 15 minutes, or until the eggs are set to your liking. Remove the pan from the oven. Switch the oven to broil. Spoon the Béchamel Sauce over the sandwiches. Return the whole pan to the oven and broil for 2 to 3 minutes, or until the Béchamel Sauce is golden and bubbly. Serve this very French sandwich with a side of creamy Dijon mustard and baby cornichons. Merci.

EGGS RABONA FRIED BREAD SANDWICHES

A traditional rabona is a fried bread sandwich—you fry the bread in oil before building your sandwich. While tasty, though, these sandwiches are rarely memorable. When playing with this recipe, I remembered a dish I used to enjoy almost weekly at a favourite Mexican restaurant: they would lay cheese flat on a grill, let it melt, and then leave it there until it charred nicely. They stopped making it and I stopped going. I thought that the thin, salty melted/fried cheese could work wonders for this sandwich, so like so many other recipes in this book, I married two amazing foods into one delicious creation. It's basically an inside-out grilled cheese sandwich.

SERVES 4

VEGETABLES . . . THEY AIN'T SO BAD, I GUESS

In a large bowl combine the cucumber, red onion, tomato, cilantro, chili pepper, lime juice, salt, and pepper. Toss to mix, then set the salad aside to allow the flavours to mingle.

Spread the Spicy Mayo on one side of each slice of bread.

FRYING CHEESE—NOW THAT'S MORE LIKE IT

Heat a large non-stick frying pan over medium heat. For each toast, sprinkle ¼ cup (60 mL) mozzarella into the frying pan in an even layer about the same size as your bread, making as many cheese layers as will fit in your pan. When the cheese has melted, place a slice of bread, Spicy Mayo side up, on top of each portion of cheese and fry for 2 minutes, or until crispy and golden brown. Flip the bread so that the crunchy, cheesy layer is on top. Fry the second side for 2 minutes, or until crispy brown. Transfer to a plate and repeat with the remaining cheese and bread.

In a medium frying pan, heat the canola oil over medium-high heat. Crack the eggs into the pan and turn the heat down to medium. Cook the eggs sunny side up for about 5 minutes.

SURPRISE, ANOTHER EGG!

To assemble, place a slice of fried bread, cheesy side down, on each plate. Drain the Vegetable Salad, then divide it evenly among the four sandwiches. Complete each sandwich with a second piece of fried bread, cheesy side up, and top with a sunny-side-up egg.

Vegetable Salad

1½ cups (375 mL) diced cucumber

1½ cups (375 mL) diced red onion

1½ cups (375 mL) diced tomatoes

¼ cup (60 mL) cilantro leaves

1 Thai red chili pepper, sliced

Juice of 1 lime

½ teaspoon (2 mL) salt

½ teaspoon (2 mL) black pepper

For Serving

1 batch Spicy Mayo (see page 41)

8 slices of your favourite soft bread

2 cups (500 mL) finely shredded mozzarella cheese, divided

2 tablespoons (30 mL) canola oil

4 large eggs

BRUNCH BURGERS

If you know anything about me, you know I'm a burger aficionado. I love, love, love a really good burger and I won't eat more than one bite of a bad one. As far as I'm concerned, a burger isn't a burger unless it has cheese and an egg on it. Together, these bring a velvety texture that ketchup and relish just can't come close to offering. This burger is one up on the good ol' Americana we serve at Lisa Marie. Wait for it . . . the egg is in the burger. That's right, *in* the burger. Mind equals blown. For these burgers, I love using ground brisket. You can go to any proper butcher and ask them to grind up some brisket for you, but if that's not available, ground chuck will do.

SERVES 2

Brunch Burger Sauce
1 dill pickle, finely diced
¼ cup (60 mL) Thousand Island dressing
1 tablespoon (15 mL) jalapeño hot sauce

Brunch Burger Patties
1 pound (450 g) coarsely ground brisket
2 teaspoons (10 mL) salt
1 teaspoon (5 mL) black pepper
1 teaspoon (5 mL) smoked paprika

For Serving
4 strips bacon, chopped into 1-inch
   (2.5 cm) pieces
2 large eggs
Salt
2 slices American cheese
2 hamburger buns, sliced in half
1 large tomato, thinly sliced
2 leaves iceberg lettuce

Make the Brunch Burger Sauce by combining the pickle, dressing, and hot sauce in a small bowl. Set aside.

REMIXIN' THE MEAT
In a large bowl combine the ground brisket, salt, pepper, and paprika. Mix well with your hands. Shape the meat into 2 patties, each just a bit wider than the hamburger buns. Poke a hole through the centre of each patty and use your fingers to widen the hole until it is about 2 inches (5 cm) wide. Set the patties aside.

Heat a non-stick frying pan over medium-high heat. Add the bacon to the hot pan and cook until it is crispy, using a wooden spoon to move the bacon around the pan so it doesn't burn. Remove the bacon from the pan and set it aside to drain on a plate lined with paper towel.

EGG IS LEGIT IN THE BURGER
In the same frying pan, cook both burger patties in the bacon fat for 3 minutes. Carefully flip the patties, then crack an egg into each hole. Season with salt and cook for another 3 minutes. Top each patty with a slice of American cheese, cover the pan, and leave on the heat for 1 to 2 minutes to allow the cheese to melt.

MESSY AS FUUUUUGH
To assemble, spread the Brunch Burger Sauce on both halves of each bun. On the bottom half of each bun, layer a few slices of tomato and a leaf of iceberg lettuce. Top with a burger-and-egg patty. Layer the bacon over the patties. Finish with the top bun.

BRUNCH BURRITOS

A brunch burrito just makes sense. I mean, think about it. Let's say you can't sit and enjoy your brunch (a sin, I'm aware). You're not going to take an order of eggs Benedict on the bus, are you? No chance! You're going for the self-contained option that can be enjoyed with one hand. This brunch burrito has all the elements you crave in a Mexican-inspired meal, tightly wrapped and grilled to seem effortless and mighty at the same time.

SERVES 2

Chunky Pepper Sauce

1 sweet green pepper

1 sweet red pepper

1 jalapeño pepper

2 cloves garlic, peeled

2 tablespoons (30 mL) canola oil, divided

1 teaspoon (5 mL) salt, divided

Juice of 1 lime

¼ cup (60 mL) cilantro leaves

1 teaspoon (5 mL) unsalted butter

Pico de Gallo

1 jalapeño pepper, finely chopped with
    seeds

1 large tomato, diced

1 cup (250 mL) diced red or white onion

¼ cup (60 mL) roughly chopped cilantro

Juice of 1 lime

1 teaspoon (5 mL) canola oil

1 teaspoon (5 mL) salt

Brunch Burritos

2 mild or spicy pork sausages

1½ teaspoons (7 mL) canola oil

4 large eggs

Salt and black pepper

1 batch Guacamole (see page 53)

2 extra-large flour tortillas
    (14 inches/35 cm or larger)

1 cup (250 mL) shredded iceberg lettuce

½ cup (125 mL) canned romano beans,
    drained and rinsed

1 cup (250 mL) grated cheddar cheese

PEPPER ROASTIN' AND BRUNCH TOASTIN'

Preheat the oven to 400°F (200°C) and line a baking sheet with parchment paper. In a large bowl combine the green pepper, red pepper, jalapeño pepper, and garlic. Drizzle with 1 tablespoon (15 mL) canola oil, sprinkle on ½ teaspoon (2 mL) salt, and toss to coat. Transfer the peppers and garlic to the prepared baking sheet and roast for 15 minutes, turning peppers once or twice while cooking. They should be fairly dark in colour and soft. Remove from the oven and carefully seed (but don't skin) the peppers.

Place the roasted peppers and garlic in a food processor and add the lime juice, cilantro, the remaining 1 tablespoon (15 mL) canola oil, and the remaining ½ teaspoon (2 mL) salt. Pulse to roughly chop the peppers and garlic (it's called "Chunky" for a reason!). Transfer the sauce to a small saucepan, add the butter, and reduce over high heat for 4 to 5 minutes. The sauce should not be watery at all, so if it needs to continue reducing in order to look chunky, go for it. Set aside the Chunky Pepper Sauce.

To make the Pico de Gallo, in a large bowl combine the jalapeño pepper, tomato, onion, cilantro, lime juice, canola oil, and salt. Set aside the Pico de Gallo to allow the flavours to mingle.

HOT SAUSAGE COMING THROUGH

Heat a frying pan over high heat. Remove the sausages from their casings and add them to the hot pan. Brown the meat for 2 minutes while breaking it apart with the back of a wooden spoon. Turn the heat down to low and continue to cook the meat for another 4 minutes.

While the sausages cook, in another medium frying pan, heat the canola oil over medium heat. Crack the eggs into a bowl and whisk until smooth. Season with salt and pepper. Pour the egg mixture into the hot pan and continue to whisk the eggs until they are fluffy and cooked.

WRAP IT UP, DUDE!

To assemble, arrange the tortillas on a work surface and spread the Guacamole among them. Then layer the lettuce, beans, cheddar, eggs, sausage, and Pico de Gallo on each wrap. Now you are ready to roll! Fold the bottom of the tortilla over the filling and use your hands to tighten the roll. Fold in both sides and continue rolling. Heat a large frying pan over high heat. When it is hot, add the burritos seam side down. Toast all sides of the burritos. Cut each burrito in half and arrange on plates. Serve with the Chunky Pepper Sauce on the side for dipping.

ROASTED TURKEY AND CHICHARRÓN CLUB

Just like my dad, I love a good diner. I live for them, actually. But unfortunately there are two types of diners out there in the world: the legitimate diners that have been around forever serving the same pies, floats, and burgers for lord knows how long, and the kind of diner that only exists to mimic the first type. How do you know which is which? Just follow my lead and order a club sandwich. Like my version here, the best ones are made with real roasted turkey (not that over-processed, overcooked stuff). You'll also find delicious bacon on a high-quality club, and this is where I've changed things up. Here the chicharróns are pseudo bacon, adding that must-have crispy, salty element. The turkey skin will shrink substantially, so if you are able to ask your butcher for more, you should!

SERVES 2

I'M A LEG GUY ALL THE WAY

Preheat the oven to 350°F (180°C). Massage the Old Bay seasoning and canola oil over all sides of the turkey thigh. Pat the meat with cornstarch, being sure to cover the skin. Place the turkey skin side up on a rack nestled into a baking sheet and roast for 2 hours, or until the internal temperature of the thigh is at least 160°F (70°C). Remove the turkey from the oven and allow it to cool to room temperature. Carefully remove the turkey skin and set it aside to make the chicharrón. Thinly slice the turkey meat. (Doing this once the meat has cooled will be much easier!)

Set the oven to broil. Place the turkey skin on the roasting rack and place in the oven for 8 to 10 minutes, until it begins to bubble and is crispy. Remove the skin from the oven, salt it lightly, and cut the chicharrón into 4 portions.

NOW GIVE IT A BOOST

Make your Spicy Mayo by mixing the mayonnaise and Sriracha in a small bowl. Toast the bread, then spread some Spicy Mayo on one side of each piece. Set aside 2 slices of toast. On each remaining slice of toast, layer tomato, lettuce, avocado, chicharrón, and sliced turkey. Stack 2 layers of sandwichy goodness to make 2 sandwiches, and top each sandwich with the reserved slice of toast, Spicy Mayo side down. Cut each sandwich in half from corner to corner, and use skewers to hold everything together. Serve any remaining Spicy Mayo on the side.

Roasted Turkey Thigh

1 tablespoon (15 mL) Old Bay seasoning

1 tablespoon (15 mL) canola oil

1 boneless, skin-on turkey thigh (3 to 5 pounds/1.4 to 2.3 kg)

1 tablespoon (15 mL) cornstarch

Salt

Spicy Mayo

⅓ cup (75 mL) mayonnaise

¼ cup (60 mL) Sriracha hot sauce

For Serving

6 slices white bread

1 tomato, thinly sliced

4 leaves iceberg lettuce

1 avocado, peeled, pitted, and thinly sliced

Brunch in San Francisco

WHEN I FIRST VISITED SAN FRANCISCO in 2009, two things struck me about the city: walking up the hills was no joke, and every restaurant sourced its ingredients from local farms. The hills, although fun, have little to do with brunch, other than it makes walking off those brunch calories a lot easier. But the food culture in San Francisco is significant, considering that in the ten years since, we've seen a surge in the farm-to-table movement across North America. San Fran pretty much wrote the book on it, and what seems to the rest of us like just another food trend has always been part of their culinary DNA. They advocate eating local not because everyone else is doing it, but because it makes a better product.

Since my first visit, trends have come and gone, but the San Francisco dining scene still emphasizes local first, everything else second. When Ky and I mapped out which cities we wanted to be a part of *Brunch Life*, San Francisco was unanimously first. A West Coast city with hippie vibes, intelligent artists, creative entrepreneurs, and an abundance of everything fresh. If that doesn't scream the makings of a brunch city, then I don't know what does.

With limited time on our hands and no idea where to eat, we crowdsourced on Facebook. Out of fifty replies, fourteen mentioned Plow. And so we found ourselves at a quaint forty-seat restaurant with massive windows, stunning hardwood floors, and an open-concept kitchen with cooks dancing around each other. We were greeted by Maxine, the owner, and sat down with her to talk about brunch culture in San Francisco and how Plow fits into that scene.

As its name suggests, the restaurant is farm-inspired and farm-driven. From day one they've worked with local producers to create a menu that reflects the seasons. The BLT—which is, by the way, amazing—will only be on the menu so long as tomatoes are in season. The scramble will only include hearty mushrooms when the farms Plow works with have access to them.

Owned by husband-and-wife team Joel Bleskacek and Maxine Siu (I feel ya, buddy), Plow is nestled on a hill in what's considered the sunniest spot in San Fran. Surrounded by a mix of homes and local shops, they are busy every day and close by two in the afternoon. Around seven thirty in the morning the lineup starts with families and strollers, by eleven it's business people, and around one the hipsters finally roll out of bed and catch the kitchen before it closes.

As we drank beer-mosas, made with local craft beer and hand-squeezed orange juice, we dug into the restaurant's namesake dish, The Plow: a beautiful plate of the freshest eggs with dark orange yolks, house-made ricotta pancakes, whipped butter, the highest-quality handmade Tamshire-breed pork sausage cakes, and house-baked rustic sourdough toast. It's simple brunch fare made exceptional by high-quality ingredients. Every bite was memorable. Then for dessert I had the avocado and egg sandwich. A must-try, considering you really don't know what a real egg yolk tastes like until you get them right from the farm. By 2:30 the busy restaurant had emptied and staff took their seats to enjoy a post-shift meal. Together as a team, they ate brunch after brunch.

It was hard to imagine what could live up to Plow, until we stumbled upon Brenda's Meat & Three. After leaving her head chef position in New Orleans, Brenda Buenviajé moved to San Francisco to work in the city's booming food scene before she opened her first restaurant, Brenda's French Soul Food, in the Tenderloin neighbourhood. Although it was in a rougher part of the city, it was all Brenda could afford at the time, but she fully intended to alter people's perceptions of the Tenderloin and to create a restaurant that people would line up for. And she did just that. Brenda has brought elevated soul food to an area not known for its restaurant scene and has been hugely successful, with lineups out the door day after day. Eight years later, Brenda opened up Brenda's Meat & Three (a southern name for a diner where you can order meat and three sides). The menu is New Orleans comfort food meets ingredient-conscious San Francisco. With a diner-style bar occupying the middle of the restaurant, Brenda's Meat & Three is comfortable, affordable, and a ritual meeting place for all avid San Fran brunchers.

We started with the incredible biscuits and homemade jam. These are clearly a crowd favourite; I watched a young couple nearby scrape the last morsel of jam out of its jar to then smear on their biscuits. Brenda served us a spread of her most beloved offerings. Calas (pronounced caw-laws) can't be found anywhere west of St. Louis, Missouri, except at Meat & Three. These fried doughnuts, made from day-old rice, are sweet, with an incredible depth of flavour. Ky and I also shared johnnycakes—cornmeal high-rise pancakes stuffed with shrimp, cheese, and three-pepper butter—alongside a plate of that New Orleans classic, shrimp and grits. By the end of the meal, I was blown away by Brenda's incomparable southern hospitality and her brunch dishes, which were literally stuck to my ribs.

Remember those hills I mentioned earlier? Well, they sure came in handy for walking off these meals.

Bennies for Brunch

IN MY HUMBLE opinion there is no single dish that screams brunch more than eggs Benedict: the velvety hollandaise sauce, the bright and ready-to-burst perfectly poached egg sitting on top of grilled ham or peameal bacon, and a lightly toasted English muffin. Four individual components that, when executed perfectly, can be incredible. I'm not going to lie. I didn't always feel this way about eggs Benny—I used to hate it. But I kept giving it a try until finally my palate caught up to my age. And now, I can't get enough Benny. Some of the most iconic brunch spots I've eaten at have a version of this dish, as does our own restaurant. We serve our Bacon Explosion Benny (page 59), and I can honestly tell you, no single item on our brunch or dinner menu is more popular. I know what you're thinking: how many variations of Benny could we possibly create? And therein lies the challenge! This chapter explores all things Benny, from the original classic, the OG Benny (page 50), to some more far-flung versions with flavours inspired by Singaporean, Argentinean, and Italian cuisine. Think of it as one big flight of Benedicts.

OG BENNY

The classic eggs Benedict. The best place to start when you're learning how to make and appreciate this dish. You can't mess with tradition until you've mastered the foundation. I know, very poetic. The single most important element of the classic is the hollandaise sauce. If it's too watery, too thick, or too sour, the entire dish is ruined. This is my go-to hollandaise recipe, and it's equally delicious in the California Benny (page 53), the Bacon Explosion Benny (page 59), and the Benny Poutine (page 66).

================= SERVES 4 =================

Hollandaise Sauce

8 large egg yolks

2 tablespoons (30 mL) fresh lemon juice

¼ cup (60 mL) unsalted butter, melted and cooled slightly

2 teaspoons (10 mL) Worcestershire sauce

4 dashes hot sauce (like Tabasco)

1 teaspoon (5 mL) white vinegar

1 teaspoon (5 mL) salt

For Serving

½ cup (125 mL) white vinegar

8 large eggs

16 slices peameal bacon

4 English muffins

2 tablespoons (30 mL) finely chopped chives, for garnish

HOLLANDAAAAAISE (SUNG LIKE MADONNA)

Fill a saucepan one-third of the way with water and bring it to a simmer. Find a heatproof bowl big enough to rest on the rim of your pot without the bottom of the bowl touching the water. Off the heat, whisk together the egg yolks and lemon juice in the bowl until the mixture doubles in size. Place the bowl over the simmering water and drizzle in the melted butter while continuously whisking. Add the butter slowly at first—if you add it too quickly, your sauce may break. Once the sauce starts to thicken, you can add the butter a little faster. Continue whisking until the hollandaise is smooth and thickened. Remove the bowl from the pot and whisk in the Worcestershire sauce, hot sauce, vinegar, and salt. If your sauce becomes too thick, add a squeeze more lemon juice to loosen it up. Leave the bowl near the warm surface of the stove but not directly on heat.

POACH, POACH, POACH, SEÑORA

Bring a wide, shallow pot of water to a slow rolling boil and add the vinegar. Crack 3 or 4 eggs into the water and poach them for 3 minutes. Using a slotted spoon, scoop the poached eggs one by one from the water and place them in a bowl of room-temperature water. Check the doneness of your eggs by gently poking them with your finger. If they feel too soft, return them to the boiling water to cook for another minute or so, then again lift them into the bowl of water. Repeat with the remaining eggs.

JUST ADD BACON

Heat a large frying pan over high heat. Add the peameal bacon in batches and fry for 2 minutes on each side or until cooked through. Transfer the cooked bacon to a plate and cover with foil or parchment paper to keep them warm while you cook the remaining slices. Lift the poached eggs from the room-temperature water with a slotted spoon and place them gently on paper towel to remove any excess moisture.

To assemble, cut the English muffins in half and toast them. Top each half with 2 slices of peameal bacon, a poached egg, and a spoonful of Hollandaise Sauce. Garnish with a sprinkling of chives.

CALIFORNIA BENNY

I consider this the equally cool vegetarian sibling of the Bacon Explosion Benny (page 59), seeing as avocado is basically a vegetarian's version of bacon. What really makes this dish stand out is how well the citrus from the guacamole and the pico de gallo pair with the hollandaise sauce. This is the go-to brunch I make for Ky at home, at the cottage, and even at the restaurant, with her personal request for the hollandaise on the side. Always on the side. You'll notice I call for farmhouse bread here, and by that I mean a healthier whole grain bread, as this recipe is a lighter vegetarian option. Feel free to use English muffins or any bread you like, but I really love using a hearty whole grain loaf.

SERVES 4

MIX IT REAL GOOD
Halve and pit the avocados and squeeze the flesh into a medium bowl. Add the cilantro and lime juice and smash with a fork to create a chunky guacamole.

CALIFORNIA BRUNCH DREAMING
To assemble, toast the farmhouse bread. Place 2 slices on each plate. Top each slice with some of the Guacamole and Pico de Gallo, a poached egg, and a spoonful of Hollandaise Sauce. Garnish with a jalapeño slice and cilantro leaves.

Guacamole
4 avocados
4 teaspoons (20 mL) chopped cilantro
Juice of 1 lime

For Serving
8 slices whole grain farmhouse bread
1 batch Pico de Gallo (see page 38)
8 poached eggs (see page 50)
1 batch Hollandaise Sauce (see page 50)
1 jalapeño pepper, sliced, for garnish
Cilantro leaves, for garnish

SINGAPORE CRAB BENNY

This dish is my best effort at marrying my two loves, Singaporean chili crab and eggs Benny. The spice and tanginess of the sauce mixed with the saltiness of the crab and the creaminess of the egg all work together perfectly. I might be biased, but this is probably my favourite dish in the entire book. And if it's not in your top five, then I don't know if we can be friends anymore.

SERVES 4

PLEASE DON'T USE IMITATION CRAB . . . IT MAKES ME SAD

Pick over the crabmeat to ensure that no shell or cartilage remains. Place the crabmeat in a medium bowl and add the garlic, chili pepper, green onion, white onion, ginger, Thai basil, and lemon zest. Mix thoroughly with your hands, breaking up the crabmeat. Add the panko and eggs and mix again. Form into 4 crab cakes, lay them on a small baking sheet, and place in the freezer for 10 minutes to help firm up the crab cakes. (You can make the Chili Sauce while the crab cakes are in the freezer.) In a wide, high-sided pan, heat the canola oil to 320°F (160°C). Remove the crab cakes from the freezer and dredge them in flour. Fry the crab cakes in batches for 2 minutes on each side. Drain on paper towels.

FEEL THE BURN

To make the Chili Sauce, in a small bowl combine the ketchup, oyster sauce, soy sauce, tamarind paste, sambal oelek, chili paste, lemon juice, green onion, and cilantro. In a small saucepan heat the canola oil over medium-high heat. Add the white onion, garlic, and ginger and sauté for 2 minutes. Stir in the ketchup mixture and cook for another minute. Remove from the heat and set aside.

HAWKER BRUNCH

Heat the canola oil in a large frying pan over medium heat. Add the watercress and sauté for 2 minutes, until the leaves wilt and the colour pops to a brighter green, then transfer to a bowl and set aside.

To assemble, place one Singapore Crab Cake on each plate. Top with sautéed watercress, a poached egg, and a spoonful of Chili Sauce. Garnish with cilantro leaves and serve remaining Chili Sauce on the side.

Singapore Crab Cakes

1½ pounds (675 g) fresh crabmeat
2 cloves garlic, minced
4 Thai red chili peppers, sliced
¼ cup (60 mL) chopped green onion
2 tablespoons (30 mL) minced white onion
2 teaspoons (10 mL) minced fresh ginger
2 teaspoons (10 mL) minced Thai basil
Grated zest of 1 lemon
1½ cups (375 mL) panko breadcrumbs
2 large eggs, lightly beaten
4 cups (1 L) canola oil
½ cup (125 mL) all-purpose flour

Chili Sauce

¼ cup (60 mL) ketchup
1 tablespoon (15 mL) oyster sauce
1 tablespoon (15 mL) soy sauce
1 tablespoon (15 mL) tamarind paste
1 tablespoon (15 mL) sambal oelek
1½ teaspoons (7 mL) chili paste
Juice of 2 lemons
1 green onion, chopped
1 tablespoon (15 mL) chopped cilantro
3 tablespoons (45 mL) canola oil
2 tablespoons (30 mL) minced white onion
4 cloves garlic, minced
1 tablespoon (15 mL) minced fresh ginger

For Serving

2 tablespoons (30 mL) canola oil
3 cups (750 mL) watercress, washed and
     dried
4 poached eggs (see page 50)
Cilantro leaves, for garnish

LAMB KEFTA BENNY

One of the most memorable meals Ky and I ever shared included a dish with lamb meatballs—it was unreal. Lamb is not a meat that's usually associated with brunch, but in my opinion, that mindset is so brunch circa 1997. For me, *Brunch Life* is all about thinking outside the box, and this recipe represents that mentality perfectly. Yes, this recipe includes poached eggs, but instead of hollandaise we've gone with a flavourful yogurt sauce and switched out English muffins for pitas. I think you'll love these meaty lamb patties, which work really well with the creaminess of the soft-poached yolk.

SERVES 4

Mediterranean Yogurt Sauce

4 cloves garlic, unpeeled
1 cup (250 mL) plain Greek yogurt
¼ cup (60 mL) finely chopped fresh curly
    parsley
1 tablespoon (15 mL) olive oil
Grated zest of 1 lemon
Salt

Lamb Kefta Patties

1 pound (450 g) ground lamb
½ cup (125 mL) diced white onion
1 teaspoon (5 mL) salt
½ teaspoon (2 mL) black pepper
½ teaspoon (2 mL) smoked paprika
½ teaspoon (2 mL) ground cumin
½ teaspoon (2 mL) onion powder
½ teaspoon (2 mL) garlic powder
¼ teaspoon (1 mL) turmeric
1 tablespoon (15 mL) canola oil

For Serving

2 large pitas
1 beefsteak tomato, sliced
4 poached eggs (see page 50)
Grated lemon zest, for garnish

ROASTED GARLIC LOVE

Preheat the oven to 400°F (200°C). Place the garlic on a small baking pan and roast for 10 minutes. Remove the roasted garlic from the oven but do not turn the oven off. Allow the garlic to cool for a minute or two until it is cool enough to handle. Peel the garlic, then smash it with the back of a knife to form a paste. In a bowl combine the smashed garlic, yogurt, parsley, olive oil, and lemon zest. Season with a pinch of salt and set aside.

IT'S A LAMB PATTY PARTY

In a medium bowl combine the ground lamb, onion, salt, pepper, paprika, cumin, onion powder, garlic powder, and turmeric. Mix well with your hands and form into 4 lamb patties. Pour the canola oil onto a paper towel and use it to grease an ovenproof grill pan. Heat the grill pan over high heat. Add the lamb patties and sear for 2 minutes on each side. Transfer the pan to the oven and roast for 6 minutes. This will cook your lamb patties to medium, so add 2 to 3 minutes if you prefer your lamb well-done.

  While the lamb patties are cooking, slice both pitas into quarters. Place these on a baking sheet and toast in the same oven you're cooking the lamb patties, for 2 to 3 minutes.

TIME TO BENNY

To assemble, lay 2 crispy pita quarters on each plate. Top with a slice of tomato, a Lamb Kefta Patty, a poached egg, and a dollop of Mediterranean Yogurt Sauce. Garnish with lemon zest and serve any remaining sauce on the side.

BACON EXPLOSION BENNY

After serving brunch at our restaurant for about a year with varying success, we sat back and scrutinized our menu, and noticed that we were doing brunch every weekend *without an eggs Benedict option*. How did we ever overlook this staple? How could our goal be to be the best brunch spot in the city if we didn't even have a Benny on the menu? Before we went ahead and did a simple eggs Benny, I looked around the kitchen to see what we had that could help make it stand out that much more. We had a lot of "bacon explosions"—bacon blankets wrapped around ground pork and smoked to perfection—left over from another event, so we cut a few up and served them with our eggs Benny. From the moment we plated our first Explosion Benny, it's been our bestselling item. It's got everything most people want in a brunch: it's hearty and filling, it's smoky and salty, it's a Benny with a twist, it sounds unreal, and it's pretty darn Instagrammable if you ask me. Call it a coincidence, but Lisa Marie has been packed for brunch ever since.

=============== SERVES 4 ===============

WEAVING YOUR BACON BLANKET

Preheat the oven to 325°F (160°C) and line a baking sheet with a large sheet of foil. Heat the canola oil in a medium frying pan over medium heat. Add the onions and cook, stirring frequently, for 6 to 7 minutes, or until caramelized. Scrape the onions into a medium bowl and add the ground pork, barbecue sauce, hot sauce, salt, and eggs. Mix well with your hands.

Lay 8 to 10 strips of bacon horizontally on the prepared baking sheet, making sure that all strips are tightly fitted together. Fold back every other strip of bacon to a little past the centre. Lay a new strip of bacon vertically on top of the horizontal strips and as close to the folded bacon as possible. Unfold the folded strips so they lie on top of the vertical strip. It will now look as though the vertical strip of bacon has been woven through the horizontal strips. Fold back the strips that weren't folded the first time, again lay a new strip of bacon vertically as close to the folded bacon as possible, and unfold the bacon. Repeat this process until half of the bacon is a tightly woven lattice. Now do the same to the other half of the bacon to complete the full bacon weave.

Mound the ground pork mixture along one long edge of the bacon weave and form it into an even log shape. Using the foil as a guide, roll the pork log forward, tightly wrapping it in the bacon blanket, but leaving the pork filling exposed at each end. With the help of the foil, transfer the roll, seam side down, onto a rack nestled into a baking sheet. (If you try to do this with just your hands, you run the risk of the roll falling apart.) Remove the foil. Bake the roll for 2 hours, until the internal temperature of the roll is at least 160°F (70°C). Set the oven to broil, transfer the roll to the lowest rack, and cook for an additional 5 minutes to crisp up the bacon.

(continues)

Bacon Explosion
2 tablespoons (30 mL) canola oil

2 cups (500 mL) thinly sliced yellow onions

2 pounds (900 g) ground pork

½ cup (125 mL) barbecue sauce

¼ cup (60 mL) vinegar-based hot sauce

2 teaspoons (10 mL) salt

3 large eggs, lightly beaten

1¾ pounds (790 g) bacon (16 to 20 strips)

For Serving
4 brioche buns

8 poached eggs (see page 50)

1 batch Hollandaise Sauce (see page 50)

¼ cup (60 mL) finely chopped chives, for garnish

Remove the Bacon Explosion from the oven and, without removing it from the rack, allow it to come to room temperature—this should take about 30 minutes. Then transfer it—still on the rack—to the fridge and cool for another 30 minutes. (This will make it much easier to slice.) Cut the Bacon Explosion into ¾-inch (2 cm) slices. Heat a medium non-stick frying pan over medium-high heat. Add the slices and cook for 1 to 2 minutes on each side to warm them through and make them crispy.

IT'S AN EXPLOSION!
To assemble, slice the brioche buns in half and toast them. Top each half bun with a bacon explosion slice, a poached egg, and 1 tablespoon (15 mL) Hollandaise Sauce. Garnish with chives.

SAUCY MEATBALL BENNY

My nonno (Italian for grandfather) was my everything. He taught me all I know, love, and appreciate about food. Once in a while, he would cook me breakfast for dinner: two sunny-side-up eggs, homemade toast (he *baked* the bread, not just put it in the toaster), and a side bowl of traditional sugo, a tomato-based sauce that is cooked for at least four hours and includes delicious chunks of tender meat. The memory of egg yolks, sugo, and fresh bread coming together will forever be etched in my mind. There's something so perfect about these flavours. Although I use glorious tender meatballs in place of my nonno's more traditional slow-cooked meat, this dish would hopefully make my nonno proud.

SERVES 4

SAUCE, RAGÙ, SUGO, GRAVY . . .

In a large pot heat the canola oil over medium-high heat. Add the onions, salt, black pepper, and chili flakes and sauté until the onions are translucent. Add the tomatoes with their liquid, stir to combine, and bring everything to a boil. Turn the heat down to medium-low and simmer the sauce, stirring occasionally, for 30 minutes, or until all the tomatoes are broken down. The sauce definitely is not done at this point, but it should be at this stage before you add the meatballs.

HOW 'BOUT DEM BALLS

Place the mushrooms and garlic in a food processor and pulse until both are finely chopped. Heat a small frying pan over medium-high heat and melt the butter. Add the mushrooms and garlic and sauté for 5 minutes. Scrape the mushroom mixture into a large bowl and add the pork, beef, eggs, panko, and salt. Mix together well with your hands, then form into 8 meatballs. Make sure that you flatten the tops and bottoms of the meatballs so a poached egg can sit on top. Heat the canola oil in a small non-stick frying pan over medium-high heat. In batches, sear the meatballs for about 2 minutes on each side. Transfer them directly into the Rustic Tomato Sauce, pushing them down gently to ensure they are fully covered in sauce. Place a lid on the pot and simmer for 2½ hours. You may need to add anywhere from ¼ to ½ cup (60 to 125 mL) of water to help loosen up the sauce if it looks too thick.

Rustic Tomato Sauce

1 tablespoon (15 mL) canola oil
1½ cups (375 mL) finely chopped yellow
   onions
½ teaspoon (2 mL) salt
½ teaspoon (2 mL) black pepper
¼ teaspoon (1 mL) chili flakes
3 cans (28 ounces/796 mL each) plum
   tomatoes

Proper Italian Meatballs

½ cup (125 mL) white button mushrooms
2 cloves garlic
4 tablespoons (60 mL) unsalted butter
½ pound (225 g) lean ground pork
½ pound (225 g) ground beef
2 large eggs, lightly beaten
¼ cup (60 mL) panko breadcrumbs
1 tablespoon (15 mL) salt
1 tablespoon (15 mL) canola oil

Garlic Bread

1 rustic ciabatta loaf
4 tablespoons (60 mL) unsalted butter,
   at room temperature
1 tablespoon (15 mL) garlic powder
1 tablespoon (15 mL) dried oregano

(continues)

For Serving

8 poached eggs (see page 50)

½ cup (125 mL) freshly grated Parmesan
   cheese

Basil leaves, for garnish

DON'T BURN THE BREAD . . . TRUST ME

Set the oven to broil. Slice the ciabatta loaf in half horizontally, butter both sides, and sprinkle with garlic powder and oregano. Place the bread on a baking sheet and broil no more than a couple of minutes, until the butter has melted and the top is crispy. Cut into 4 portions.

To assemble, place a portion of garlic bread on each plate. Top each with 2 saucy meatballs and 2 poached eggs. Sprinkle Parmesan over top and garnish with basil leaves.

CHORIZO AND TOSTONES BENNY

What I love about this chapter is that once you have your eggs Benny base down, you can start creating really fun iterations of the dish. That's how we came up with many of these recipes. Instead of bread, this Cubano take on eggs Benny includes tostones, which are thick-cut plantains that have been fried once, smashed flat, and then fried again. Lightly salted, these are amazing served with chimichurri (see page 12) or salsa verde. The homemade chorizo patties are a smoky contrast to the more subtle flavours of the traditional eggs Benny. From top to bottom we see a very pronounced flavour profile: an elevated hollandaise, a hearty, spicy chorizo patty, and then a completely different vessel to soak it all up.

======================= SERVES 4 =======================

THE TOSTONES ON YOU

In a large saucepan over medium-high heat, heat the canola oil to 350°F (180°C). Fry the plantain medallions for 3 minutes, working in batches if necessary. Remove from the oil and drain on paper towels. Flatten each medallion with a spatula or a heavy, flat-bottomed glass. Return smashed plantains to the oil and fry for another 2 minutes. Drain again, transfer to a large bowl, and toss with kosher salt.

OH, CHORIZO, YOU'RE MY HERO

While the tostones are frying, preheat the oven to 350°F (180°C). Remove the sausages from their casings, and in a large bowl combine the sausage meat, garlic powder, onion powder, paprika, and pepper. Mix well with your hands and form into 8 patties. Heat a large cast-iron frying pan over high heat. Add the butter, and when it has melted, sear the patties for 1 minute on each side. Transfer the pan to the oven and bake for 5 minutes to finish cooking.

GIVE THAT HOLLY A LITTLE OOMPH

Set the oven to broil. Place the jalapeño peppers on a small baking sheet and broil for 5 to 8 minutes, turning once while cooking, until they begin to char. Put the jalapeño peppers in a food processor and add the cilantro, canola oil, and lemon juice. Blend into a fine paste. Make the Hollandaise Sauce, then fold the cilantro paste into the finished sauce. Place the bowl on the warm cook surface but not directly on heat.

To assemble, place 2 Tostones on each plate and top each with a Chorizo Sausage Patty (or place the Tostones on top of the patties). Place a poached egg on top of each patty, and spoon over 1 tablespoon (15 mL) Spicy Hollandaise Sauce. Garnish with cilantro leaves.

Tostones
1 cup (250 mL) canola oil

2 green plantains, peeled and cut diagonally into 8 (1-inch/2.5 cm) medallions

1 teaspoon (5 mL) kosher salt

Chorizo Sausage Patties
1¾ pounds (790 g) mild Italian sausage

1 tablespoon (15 mL) garlic powder

1 tablespoon (15 mL) onion powder

2 teaspoons (10 mL) smoked paprika

½ teaspoon (2 mL) black pepper

1 tablespoon (15 mL) unsalted butter

Spicy Hollandaise Sauce
2 jalapeño peppers

¼ cup (60 mL) cilantro leaves

2 tablespoons (30 mL) canola oil

Juice of 1 lemon

1 batch Hollandaise Sauce (see page 50)

For Serving
8 poached eggs (see page 50)

Cilantro leaves, for garnish

BENNY POUTINE

I'm just going to come out and say it: I've never been a massive fan of poutine. I get why people like it and I understand why it's so popular, but what bothers me about the dish is that the fries are rarely crispy and the gravy either tastes synthetic or isn't hot enough to melt the curds. That being said, I thought it could be fun to make a brunch Benny version, substituting hollandaise and runny egg yolks for the gravy and ensuring the fries were more thick wedges than thin frites. But I've made sure the cheese curds are legit. If they weren't legit, the poutine police would call bullshit on this recipe. Don't believe me? Head over to the Fidel Gastro YouTube channel and read the comments under my Irish Poutine video. I used white cheddar. Nonstop heckling.

SERVES 4

Thick-Cut French Fries

5 skin-on russet potatoes, washed

8 cups (2 L) canola oil

¼ cup (60 mL) cornstarch

2 sprigs fresh rosemary

1 teaspoon (5 mL) kosher salt

For Serving

½ cup (125 mL) white vinegar

4 large eggs

8 ounces (225 g) cheese curds

1 batch Hollandaise Sauce (see page 50)

¼ cup (60 mL) finely chopped chives, for garnish

THICK-CUT FRIES MEET ALL THE BEST THINGS

Cut the potatoes into 1-inch (2.5 cm) thick fries (almost like wedges!) and place them in a large pot. Cover them with cold water, bring to a boil, and blanch for 10 minutes. While the potatoes are blanching, in a large, deep pot over medium-high heat, heat the oil to 350°F (180°C).

Drain the potatoes and immediately submerge them in an ice bath to stop cooking. Drain the potatoes again, lay them out on a baking sheet, and pat dry. Place the dried potatoes in a large bowl, sprinkle with cornstarch, and toss to coat. Working in batches, carefully add the potatoes to the hot oil and fry for 12 minutes, or until golden brown and crispy. During the last 2 minutes of frying, add the rosemary sprigs to the pot. Remove the potatoes and rosemary from the oil and drain them of excess oil on paper towel. Place them in a large bowl and crumble the fried rosemary over the potatoes, add the salt, and toss well.

While the potatoes are frying, bring a wide, shallow pot of water to a slow, rolling boil and add the vinegar. Crack the eggs into the water and poach them for 3 minutes. Using a slotted spoon, scoop the poached eggs one by one from the water and place them in a bowl of room-temperature water. Check the doneness of your eggs by gently poking them with your finger. If they feel too soft, return them to the boiling water to cook for another 1 to 2 minutes, then again lift them into the bowl of water. Lift the poached eggs from the room-temperature water with a slotted spoon and place them gently on a paper towel to remove any excess moisture.

To assemble, arrange the Thick-Cut French Fries on a platter and top with the cheese curds, poached eggs, and Hollandaise Sauce. Sprinkle with chives and serve family style for sharing.

Brunch in Seattle

WHEN A CITY TRANSFORMS, can it really shed all of its old identity? I knew very little about Seattle before Ky and I visited, other than that it was the birthplace of grunge music in the early '90s and it's the city where the TV show *Frasier* is set. That's pretty much it. Despite my lack of knowledge, though, I've never felt so at home in a city. We walked everywhere, checked out Pike Place Market (the birthplace of Starbucks coffee), and visited the fish markets where we ate smoked salmon right on the water. Every meal we had was exceptional; the restaurants serve food that is innovative and unique and embraces local ingredients. As amazing as Seattle is, I had a hard time believing that we were in the birthplace of Jimi Hendrix and bands like Nirvana and Pearl Jam. How did this walkable, clean, and trendy city foster an environment for "Smells Like Teen Spirit", ripped jeans, and grunge rock?

And then we visited Beth's Cafe, home to the legendary Triple Bypass twelve-egg omelette. As our Uber driver took us down Aurora Avenue, we quickly saw the Seattle of old. The Seattle that gave birth to one of the most rebellious forms of rock music of all time. There's no two ways of saying it: Beth's has always been a grungy diner with a smile. A purple facade, crayon drawings on the wall, open twenty-four hours a day for the last fifty-four years, and peak business hours starting at two in the morning. It opened in the 1950s as a slot machine hub that served hash browns to keep people gambling. Musicians spurred the diner's cult mystique, as they would pour in by the busload after their shows and eat lots and lots of eggs, swear, and smoke. It was a reflection of the times and of previous decades—the '70s, '80s, and '90s—when culture was created, instead of trends being followed. These musicians didn't want lobster and brown M&M's after they played; they wanted bacon and cigarettes, and they wanted to drink from the bottles of bourbon they walked in with.

As times changed, so did Beth's offerings. Today, the diner is proudly owned by Chris Dalton, and in all honesty, I've never met someone more proud of owning a greasy spoon. He embraces it wholeheartedly, although a recent addition to the menu includes—wait for it— fresh fruit. In a city where restaurants compete at having the best relationships with farmers and fishermen, in a comical turn, Chris is just impressed with himself for concluding that some people might want some fruit with all the meat and heart attack-worthy food they are about to crush.

To put things into perspective, Beth's goes through 450,000 eggs and 52 tons of hash browns *every year*. Putting it mildly, the menu has shock value. I ate (almost ate . . . more like dented) The Triple Bypass, an omelette that is served on a pizza pan, is made with a dozen eggs, and contains one pound of cheese, bacon, ham, and sausage. Oh, and it comes with a mound of home fries. Washing it down with juice clearly wasn't an option—they didn't have juice, nor did I want any—so when a milkshake consisting of brownies and bacon became my "beverage," I immediately got sweaty just wondering how anyone could finish all that. I ambitiously attempted to make Chris proud by cleaning my plate, but as you might expect, both he and I knew it was never going to happen. Let's just say dishes like this are best shared.

This may not be the most elegant meal we feature in the book, but it personifies the community element of brunch, and Beth's has been doing that since long before brunch was even a word. While the Seattle dining scene has evolved into a trendy foodie experience, Beth's proudly exemplifies a fuck you to that.

Brunch
Is Chicken and
Waffles

THERE'S NO DISH I'm more enamoured of than fried chicken and waffles. The first time I heard of it my jaw dropped—what a genius combination! The crisp fried batter holds in all that tender chicken, piping hot, perched on a fluffy waffle. The waffle not only absorbs all the hot grease from the fried chicken but also catches the maple syrup or hot sauce (or both) you pour over top. When I started seeing more and more places doing chicken and waffles in Toronto, I knew that brunch was becoming a real thing. It was the end of dainty omelettes and your choice of sausage, bacon, or ham. This dish single-handedly made me passionate about brunch—lining up for it, eating it, and then ultimately cooking it for others. So naturally I had to devote an entire chapter to my favourite meal. My challenge: how exactly to transform this seemingly simple concept of fried chicken + waffle = awesome. It was pretty straightforward, actually: a waffle doesn't have to be just a waffle, and fried chicken is way more than breaded chicken. This is one of the most fun chapters in *Brunch Life*, and I really pushed the boundaries of what chicken and waffles can mean. I played with different sauces, like tandoori butter with my Tandoori Fried Chicken and Chickpea Waffles (page 82) and Nashville-style spicy butter in Hot Chicken and Waffles (page 78). I flavoured the fried chicken dredges, incorporating Filipino flavour in Adobo Chicken and Waffles (page 81) and popcorn seasoning in Popcorn Chicken and Waffle Bits (page 92). And I even went to the lengths of using cauliflower in my Saucy Fried Cauliflower and Green Onion Waffles (page 95).

Frying Chicken 101

THERE REALLY IS an art to frying chicken, especially if you want the crispiest, juiciest piece of meat possible. I swear by a deep-fryer, whether in the Lisa Marie kitchen or my own. Some great countertop deep-fryers are available, and I rely on these when cooking up fried chicken at home.

Knowing full well that not everyone has a deep-fryer, all these recipes can also be made in a large pot of hot oil. Here are some pointers for deep-frying in a pot.

- Choose a large pot or Dutch oven, one that will be able to hold enough oil to most effectively simulate a deep-fryer. Pots can vary in size, so while I recommend 16 cups (4 L) of oil, if your pot isn't big enough, use less oil, and fry your chicken in batches.
- That said, you don't want too *little* oil in the pot. The key to perfect fried chicken is fully submerging the entire piece of chicken in the oil. Use enough oil in your pot so you don't have to keep flipping the chicken from one side to the other in the oil, which results in the delicious coating falling off.
- You also don't want too *much* oil in the pot. Unlike a countertop deep-fryer, a pot doesn't have a fill line. Be careful that you don't fill the pot too full, otherwise oil may spill out when you add the chicken.
- Have baking soda on hand, in case any oil makes its way out of the pot and onto your hot elements. A dump of baking soda can be used to stop a small grease fire.
- Unlike a deep-fryer, a pot obviously doesn't come with a built-in thermometer, so make sure to invest in one and keep an eye on the heat—you don't want to burn the outside or undercook the inside of the chicken.

Happy frying!

HOT CHICKEN AND WAFFLES

I'd heard of Nashville hot chicken before I'd visited the city, and thought it was just another name for fried chicken. Trying it for the first time, I found it altogether different from what I expected. And by different, I mean awesome. As the name reveals, hot chicken is incredibly hot—as in spicy. The chicken is dredged and fried in oil, as usual, but to finish it off, it's painted with a cayenne spiced butter. Traditionally it's paired with butter pickles and tops a slice of white bread to soak up all the spicy juices. In my twist, I've used the white bread as the base of the waffle.

SERVES 4

Hot Chicken

1 whole chicken, cut into 8 pieces
3 cups (750 mL) buttermilk
16 cups (4 L) canola oil
3 cups (750 mL) all-purpose flour
1 teaspoon (5 mL) salt
1 teaspoon (5 mL) black pepper

White Bread Waffles

16 slices soft white bread
4 large eggs, lightly beaten
1 cup (250 mL) buttermilk
1 teaspoon (5 mL) salt

Hot Butter

½ cup (125 mL) unsalted butter
1 teaspoon (5 mL) salt
1 teaspoon (5 mL) onion powder
½ teaspoon (2 mL) mango habanero
    seasoning
½ teaspoon (2 mL) cayenne pepper
½ teaspoon (2 mL) chili powder

For Garnish

12 slices bread and butter pickles

BATTER AND FRY

Place the chicken pieces in a large bowl and cover with the buttermilk. Cover and refrigerate for at least 1 hour. Fill a deep-fryer or large pot with canola oil and heat to 350°F (180°C). See page 76 for instructions and tips on how to best fry chicken in a large pot.

In another large bowl stir together the flour, salt and pepper. Remove the chicken from the buttermilk one piece at a time and dredge it in the seasoned flour. Give each piece of chicken a good squeeze to ensure it is covered in flour and the coating is packed tightly. The more packed it is, the crispier the chicken will be. Place the chicken in the fryer or pot and cook for 15 minutes, until you have a super crispy golden brown exterior. Use a meat thermometer to ensure the internal temperature of the chicken is at least 160°F (70°C). Drain the chicken on paper towels.

WHITE BREAD IN WAFFLE FORM

Preheat a non-stick waffle iron. Rip the white bread into small pieces and place in a large bowl. Add the eggs, buttermilk, and salt and stir to combine. Grease the waffle iron, ladle in the batter, and cook for 5 minutes, or until the waffles are golden brown. Repeat to make 4 waffles.

WHAT SEPARATES THE FRIED FROM THE HOT

In a medium saucepan melt the butter, then add the salt, onion powder, mango habanero seasoning, cayenne pepper, and chili powder; whisk thoroughly. Remove from the heat and whisk again.

To assemble, brush the Hot Butter over the fried chicken (or dip the chicken in the butter using a pair of tongs). Place a White Bread Waffle on each plate and top each with 2 pieces of Hot Chicken. For a traditional touch, garnish with bread and butter pickles.

ADOBO CHICKEN AND WAFFLES

I've been fortunate to work with an amazing local talent, Ray Ligaya, on the Fidel Gastro YouTube channel. Ray is Filipino, and during this creative endeavour, he asked if I could create a brunch dish that spoke to his culture. It just so happens that fried chicken is also one of his favourite dishes, so I thought I'd riff off that traditional Filipino dish of chicken adobo and do a fried chicken and sour cream waffles version. Adobo really is the perfect blend of salty, spicy, and garlicky, and I love how these Southeast Asian flavours transform this classic southern dish.

=========== SERVES 4 ===========

BATTER AND FRY

Place the chicken pieces in a large bowl and cover with the buttermilk. Cover and refrigerate for at least 1 hour. Fill a deep-fryer or large pot with canola oil and heat to 350°F (180°C). See page 76 for instructions and tips on how to best fry chicken in a large pot.

In another large bowl stir together the flour, salt, chili pepper, and onion powder. Remove the chicken from the buttermilk one piece at a time and dredge it in the seasoned flour. Give each piece of chicken a good squeeze to ensure it is covered in flour and the coating is packed tightly. The more packed it is, the crispier the chicken will be. Place the chicken in the fryer or pot and cook for 15 minutes, until you have a super crispy golden brown exterior. Use a meat thermometer to ensure the internal temperature of the chicken is at least 160°F (70°C). Drain the chicken on paper towels.

ADOBO TIME

Melt the butter in a medium saucepan over medium heat. Stir in the garlic, chili flakes, and soy sauce and simmer for 5 minutes. Add the maple syrup and continue to simmer for 2 minutes more, or until the adobo sauce has a slightly thicker consistency. You should be able to easily run a spoon through it but it should also stick to the spoon.

SWEET, SOME SOUR CREAM WAFFLES

Preheat a non-stick waffle iron. In a large bowl whisk together the flour, baking powder, sugar, salt, cinnamon, and ginger; stir in the green onion. In a separate bowl whisk together the eggs, sour cream, and butter. Add the wet ingredients to the dry ingredients and stir until the batter is smooth. Grease the waffle iron, ladle in batter, and cook for 5 minutes, or until the waffles are golden brown. Repeat to make 4 waffles.

To assemble, place a Sour Cream Waffle on each plate and top each with 2 pieces of Adobo Fried Chicken. Drizzle Adobo Syrup over the chicken and garnish with a sprinkle of green onion. Serve any remaining Adobo Syrup on the side for dipping.

Adobo Fried Chicken

1 whole chicken, cut into 8 pieces
3 cups (750 mL) buttermilk
16 cups (4 L) canola oil
3 cups (750 mL) all-purpose flour
1 teaspoon (5 mL) salt
1 teaspoon (5 mL) chopped Thai red chili
    pepper
1 teaspoon (5 mL) onion powder

Adobo Syrup

3 tablespoons (45 mL) unsalted butter
6 cloves garlic, finely chopped
2 teaspoons (10 mL) chili flakes
¾ cup (175 mL) soy sauce
¾ cup (175 mL) pure maple syrup

Sour Cream Waffles

4 cups (1 L) all-purpose flour
2 tablespoons (30 mL) baking powder
2 teaspoons (10 mL) white sugar
2 teaspoons (10 mL) salt
1 teaspoon (5 mL) cinnamon
1 teaspoon (5 mL) ground ginger
1 cup (250 mL) finely chopped green
    onion
4 large eggs
2 cups (500 mL) sour cream
¾ cup (175 mL) unsalted butter, melted

For Garnish

¼ cup (60 mL) sliced green onion

TANDOORI FRIED CHICKEN AND CHICKPEA WAFFLES

Coming up with chicken and waffle combinations was more fun than we thought it would be. Once the classics were out of the way, we were able to brainstorm out-of-the-box flavour combinations. I wasn't sure how this dish would go over when recipe testing, but lo and behold, this was almost a unanimous favourite. It's hearty, buttery, and smoky, with a wonderful array of flavours from the vibrant Indian spices.

=== SERVES 4 ===

Tandoori Fried Chicken

1 whole chicken, cut into 8 pieces

3 cups (750 mL) buttermilk

16 cups (4 L) canola oil

3 cups (750 mL) all-purpose flour

1 teaspoon (5 mL) salt

1 tablespoon (15 mL) smoked paprika

1 tablespoon (15 mL) garam masala

1 teaspoon (5 mL) ground ginger

1 teaspoon (5 mL) ground cumin

½ teaspoon (2 mL) turmeric

Chickpea Waffles

4 cups (1 L) all-purpose flour

2 tablespoons + 2 teaspoons (40 mL)
    baking powder

1 tablespoon (15 mL) tandoori spice

2 teaspoons (10 mL) white sugar

½ teaspoon (2 mL) salt

¼ cup (60 mL) finely chopped green
    onion

3½ cups (875 mL) 2% or whole milk

4 large eggs

¼ cup (60 mL) mango chutney

1 can (19 ounces/540 mL) chickpeas,
    drained and rinsed (about
    2 cups/500 mL)

Tandoori Butter Sauce

½ cup (125 mL) unsalted butter

1 tablespoon (15 mL) tandoori spice

For Garnish

¼ cup (60 mL) sliced green onion

½ cup (125 mL) mango chutney, warmed

SURPRISE, FRY MORE CHICKEN

Place the chicken pieces in a large bowl and cover with the buttermilk. Cover and refrigerate for at least 1 hour. Fill a deep-fryer or large pot with canola oil and heat to 350°F (180°C). See page 76 for instructions and tips on how to best fry chicken in a large pot.

In another large bowl whisk together the flour, salt, paprika, garam masala, ginger, cumin, and turmeric. Remove the chicken from the buttermilk one piece at a time and dredge it in the seasoned flour. Give each piece of chicken a good squeeze to ensure it is covered in flour and the coating is packed tightly. The more packed it is, the crispier the chicken will be. Place the chicken in the fryer or pot and cook for 15 minutes, until you have a super crispy golden brown exterior. Use a meat thermometer to ensure the internal temperature of the chicken is at least 160°F (70°C). Drain the chicken on paper towels.

HOW MUCH CHIC PEA IS TOO MUCH CHIC PEA

Preheat a non-stick waffle iron. In a large bowl whisk together the flour, baking powder, tandoori spice, sugar, and salt; stir in the green onion. In a separate bowl whisk together the milk, eggs, and mango chutney. Add the wet ingredients to the dry ingredients and stir until the batter is smooth. Fold in the chickpeas. Grease the waffle iron, ladle in the batter, and cook for 5 minutes, or until the waffles are golden brown. Repeat to make 4 waffles.

TANDOORI BUTTER TIME

While the waffles are cooking, melt the butter in a medium saucepan over medium heat. Stir in the tandoori spice.

To assemble, brush the chicken with the Tandoori Butter Sauce (or dip the chicken into the sauce using a pair of tongs). Place a Chickpea Waffle on each plate and top each with 2 pieces of Tandoori Fried Chicken. Garnish with a sprinkling of green onion and a drizzle of warm mango chutney.

CAROLINA FRIED CHICKEN THIGHS
AND SPICY MINI BISCUIT WAFFLES

There are two kinds of people in this world: those who like mustard and those who don't. For this recipe you have to love mustard. If you drive down to the barbecue belt in the southern U.S., every state is known for doing barbecue their own specific way. Some use a vinegar-based sauce, others use a sweeter brown sugar–based sauce, some use molasses, and in South Carolina, they use mustard—it's even called Carolina gold sauce. This recipe takes two staples of the South—biscuits and gold sauce—and turns them into one epic brunch sandwich. The two work so well together: the super-buttery biscuit waffle coupled with hot and crispy fried chicken and the tanginess of the mustard barbecue sauce. Hand. Held. Perfection.

=================== SERVES 4 TO 6 ===================

CRISPY THIGHS

Place the chicken thighs in a large bowl and cover with the buttermilk. Cover and refrigerate for at least 1 hour. Fill a deep-fryer or large pot with canola oil and heat to 350°F (180°C). See page 76 for instructions and tips on how to best fry chicken in a large pot.

In another large bowl whisk together the flour, onion powder, salt, and pepper. Remove the chicken from the buttermilk one piece at a time and dredge it in the seasoned flour. Give each piece of chicken a good squeeze to ensure it is covered in flour and the coating is packed tightly. The more packed it is, the crispier the chicken will be. Place the chicken in the fryer or pot and cook for 12 minutes. Use a meat thermometer to ensure the internal temperature of the chicken is at least 160°F (70°C). Drain the chicken on paper towels.

VEGETABLES IN YOUR FRIED CHICKEN?

Make the Broccoli and Cranberry Slaw while the chicken marinates. In a medium bowl combine the broccoli, carrot, cranberries, mayonnaise, salt, vinegar, and hot sauce. Mix thoroughly and set the slaw aside in the refrigerator to allow flavours to mingle.

To make the Carolina Sauce, in a medium bowl whisk together the mustard, maple syrup, balsamic vinegar, and paprika. Set aside the sauce.

Fried Chicken Thighs

6 boneless, skinless chicken thighs

3 cups (750 mL) buttermilk

16 cups (4 L) canola oil

3 cups (750 mL) all-purpose flour

1 teaspoon (5 mL) onion powder

1 teaspoon (5 mL) salt

½ teaspoon (2 mL) black pepper

Broccoli and Cranberry Slaw

2 small bunches broccoli, cut into florets
    and then into matchsticks

1 large carrot, grated

½ cup (125 mL) dried cranberries

3 tablespoons (45 mL) mayonnaise

1 teaspoon (5 mL) salt

1 teaspoon (5 mL) white vinegar

1 teaspoon (5 mL) Buffalo-style hot sauce

Carolina Sauce

1 cup (250 mL) yellow mustard

½ cup (125 mL) pure maple syrup

1 tablespoon (15 mL) balsamic vinegar

¼ teaspoon (1 mL) paprika

(continues)

Spicy Mini Biscuit Waffles

2 cups (500 mL) all-purpose flour

1 tablespoon (15 mL) white sugar

1 tablespoon (15 mL) baking powder

1 teaspoon (5 mL) salt

⅓ cup (75 mL) vegetable shortening, frozen

1 cup (250 mL) 2% or whole milk

3 tablespoons (45 mL) Buffalo-style hot sauce

TIME TO BISCUIT, BABY

Preheat a non-stick waffle iron. In a large bowl whisk together the flour, sugar, baking powder, and salt. Use the large holes of a cheese grater to grate the frozen shortening into the dry ingredients. Crumble the grated shortening and flour together with your fingers until the mixture resembles pea-size crumbles. Add the milk and hot sauce and stir to form a dough. Using your hands, form the dough into 12 balls about the size of a golf ball (about 1 ounce/30 g each). Grease the waffle iron and put 1 dough ball in each of your waffle iron's sections, far enough apart that the waffles won't touch. Cook for 6 minutes, or until the waffles are golden brown. Repeat until you have 12 mini waffles.

SAUCE IT UP

Dip all the Fried Chicken Thighs into the Carolina Sauce. To assemble, place 6 Spicy Mini Biscuit Waffles on a platter. Top each with a chicken thigh and ¼ cup (60 mL) Broccoli and Cranberry Slaw. Sandwich with another Spicy Mini Biscuit Waffle. It may help to skewer your mini sandwiches!

COCONUT FRIED CHICKEN AND PINEAPPLE WAFFLES

I created this fried chicken and waffle combo for Ky. She loves pineapple on pizza. Me? Not so much. But I respect anyone who can stomach it. Pineapple in a waffle, though—now that makes a lot more sense. Beneath the coconut fried chicken sit these juicy waffles with almost candy-like little pockets that explode with tropical flavour. Because the pineapple is so sweet, I needed to make sure the coconut flavour was evenly balanced. Mixing shredded coconut into the batter didn't do it justice, so I upped the coconut quotient by swapping out the traditional buttermilk for coconut milk to marinate the chicken. This almost smoky coconut flavour subtly permeates the meat. It's like your mouth went on an all-inclusive Caribbean cruise.

SERVES 4

SURPRISE! MORE FRIED CHICKEN

Place the chicken pieces in a large bowl and cover with the coconut milk. Cover and refrigerate for at least 1 hour. Fill a deep-fryer or large pot with canola oil and heat to 350°F (180°C). See page 76 for instructions and tips on how to best fry chicken in a large pot.

Place the shredded coconut in a food processor and process it until it is the consistency of flour. In a large bowl whisk together the coconut, flour, and salt. Remove the chicken from the coconut milk one piece at a time and dredge it in the flour mixture. Give each piece of chicken a good squeeze to ensure it is covered in flour and the coating is packed tightly. The more packed it is, the crispier the chicken will be. Place the chicken in the fryer or pot and cook for 15 minutes, until you have a super crispy golden brown exterior. Use a meat thermometer to ensure the internal temperature of the chicken is at least 160°F (70°C). Drain the chicken on paper towels and season with salt.

PINEAPPLE, MEET SYRUP. SYRUP, MEET PINEAPPLE.

Make the Pineapple Syrup while the chicken marinates. Drain the crushed pineapple, reserving the pineapple for the waffles. Pour 1 cup (250 mL) pineapple juice into a small saucepan and bring it to a simmer over medium-low heat. Simmer until reduced by one-quarter, about 5 minutes. Stir in the maple syrup. Simmer until again reduced by a quarter, about 10 minutes. Transfer the Pineapple Syrup to a bowl and place it in the refrigerator to cool for 30 minutes.

Coconut Fried Chicken

1 whole chicken, cut into 8 pieces

3 cups (750 mL) coconut milk

16 cups (4 L) canola oil

1 cup (250 mL) unsweetened shredded coconut

2 cups (500 mL) all-purpose flour

1 teaspoon (5 mL) salt

Pineapple Syrup

1 can (14 ounces/398 mL) crushed pineapple

½ cup (125 mL) pure maple syrup

Pineapple Waffles

4 cups (1 L) all-purpose flour

2 tablespoons + 2 teaspoons (40 mL) baking powder

2 teaspoons (10 mL) white sugar

½ teaspoon (2 mL) salt

3½ cups (875 mL) 2% or whole milk

4 large eggs

(continues)

IF YOU LIKE PINEAPPLE WAFFLES . . . (SUNG LIKE THE JIMMY BUFFETT SONG)

Preheat a non-stick waffle iron. In a large mixing bowl combine the flour, baking powder, sugar, and salt. In a separate bowl, whisk together the milk, eggs, and the reserved crushed pineapple. Add the wet ingredients to the dry ingredients and mix until the batter is smooth. Grease the waffle iron, ladle in the batter and cook for about 5 minutes or until golden brown. Repeat to make 4 waffles.

DRIZZLE AS YOU LIKE

To assemble, place a Pineapple Waffle on each plate and top each with 2 pieces of Coconut Fried Chicken. Drizzle the Pineapple Syrup over the chicken and serve the remaining syrup on the side.

FRIED CORNISH HEN AND CORNBREAD WAFFLES

When we started doing brunch at Lisa Marie, I knew we had to include a chicken and waffle dish unique to our establishment, but not a complete departure from the classic. And thus, the creation of this recipe. Cornish hen is the ideal poultry for frying because of its smaller size. Hens cook evenly, as opposed to a standard chicken, which has a much larger breast than thigh and so you run the risk of overcooking one part but undercooking the other. With this perfectly fried hen comes a cornbread waffle. The cornbread batter is denser and heartier than your typical waffle, and really makes this dish sing. And just like we do at Lisa Marie, I love serving this with a side of spicy maple syrup.

SERVES 4

THE HEN IS GAME

Place the hen halves in a large bowl and cover with the buttermilk. Cover and refrigerate for at least 1 hour. Fill a deep-fryer or large pot with canola oil and heat to 350°F (180°C). See page 76 for instructions and tips on how to best fry chicken in a large pot.

In another large bowl whisk together the flour, garlic powder, salt, and paprika. Remove the hen from the buttermilk one piece at a time and dredge it in the seasoned flour. Give each hen half a good squeeze to ensure it is covered in flour and the coating is packed tightly. The more packed it is, the crispier the chicken will be. Place the hen pieces in the fryer or pot and cook for 15 minutes, until you have a super crispy golden brown exterior. Use a meat thermometer to ensure the internal temperature of the chicken is at least 160°F (70°C). Drain the Cornish hens on paper towels and season with salt.

ONE HEARTY WAFFLE

Preheat a non-stick waffle iron. In a large bowl whisk together the flour, cornmeal, baking powder, sugar, and salt. In a separate bowl whisk together the buttermilk, milk, and eggs. Add the wet ingredients to the dry ingredients and stir until the batter is smooth. Fold in the jalapeño peppers. Grease the waffle iron, ladle in the batter, and cook for 6 to 7 minutes, or until the waffles are golden brown. Repeat to make 4 waffles.

To make the Spicy Maple Syrup, stir together the maple syrup and hot sauce in a small bowl.

SERVE IT UP JUST LIKE WE DO AT LISA MARIE

To assemble, place a Cornbread Waffle on each plate and top each with one half of a Fried Cornish Hen. Serve with a side of Spicy Maple Syrup.

Fried Cornish Hen

2 Cornish hens, halved lengthwise
4 cups (1 L) buttermilk
16 cups (4 L) canola oil
3 cups (750 mL) all-purpose flour
2 tablespoons (30 mL) garlic powder
1 teaspoon (5 mL) salt
1 teaspoon (5 mL) paprika

Cornbread Waffles

2 cups (500 mL) all-purpose flour
2 cups (500 mL) cornmeal
2 tablespoons + 2 teaspoons (40 mL) baking powder
2 teaspoons (10 mL) white sugar
½ teaspoon (2 mL) salt
2 cups (500 mL) buttermilk
1½ cups (375 mL) 2% or whole milk
4 large eggs
2 jalapeño peppers, sliced

Spicy Maple Syrup

1 cup (250 mL) pure maple syrup
½ cup (125 mL) habanero hot sauce

POPCORN CHICKEN AND WAFFLE BITS

All the other chicken and waffle recipes in this chapter are quite . . . filling. And rightfully so! Chicken and waffles is meant to be over the top and maybe even your only meal of the day. This is a fun version that is more snack size. Brunch and a movie, perhaps, or a little midday brunch soirée, or cute little brunch canapés? And let's not forget sleepover snacks for the kids. I would have totally crushed these growing up.

SERVES 4

Popcorn Fried Chicken

16 cups (4 L) canola oil

2 large eggs

1 cup (250 mL) buttermilk

2 boneless, skinless chicken breasts, cut
    into 1-inch (2.5 cm) pieces

1 cup (250 mL) all-purpose flour

1 teaspoon (5 mL) salt

1 teaspoon (5 mL) garlic powder

Waffle Bits

1 cup (250 mL) all-purpose flour

2 teaspoons (10 mL) baking powder

½ teaspoon (2 mL) white sugar

¼ teaspoon (1 mL) salt

¾ cup (175 mL) 2% or whole milk

1 egg

Spicy Butter Topping

½ cup (125 mL) unsalted butter

¼ cup (60 mL) pure maple syrup

¼ cup (60 mL) Sriracha hot sauce

For Serving

2 cups (500 mL) popped popcorn

ITTY BITTY CHICKY

Fill a deep-fryer or large pot with canola oil and heat to 350°F (180°C). See page 76 for instructions and tips on how to best fry chicken in a large pot.

In a medium bowl whisk the eggs with the buttermilk. Place the chicken pieces in the egg mixture, making sure they are fully submerged. In another large bowl whisk together the flour, salt, and garlic powder. Working in batches if you need to, remove the chicken pieces from the egg mixture and dredge them in the seasoned flour. Give each piece of chicken a good squeeze to ensure it is covered in flour and the coating is packed tightly. The more packed it is, the crispier the chicken will be. Place the chicken in the fryer or pot and cook for 10 minutes, until you have a super crispy golden brown exterior. Drain the chicken on paper towels and season with salt.

WAFFLE BITS

Preheat a non-stick waffle iron. In a large bowl whisk together the flour, baking powder, sugar, and salt. In a separate bowl, whisk together the milk and egg. Add the wet ingredients to the dry ingredients and stir until the batter is smooth. Grease the waffle iron, ladle in the batter, and cook for 5 minutes, or until the waffles are golden brown. If needed, repeat with the remaining batter. Let the waffles cool on a rack for about 1 minute, then tear them into bite-size pieces.

BRUNCHIN' AND POPPIN'

Melt the butter in a medium saucepan over medium heat. Stir in the maple syrup and Sriracha.

In a large bowl toss together the Popcorn Fried Chicken, Waffle Bits, popcorn, and a drizzle of Spicy Butter Topping. Divide among 4 bowls and serve.

SAUCY FRIED CAULIFLOWER AND GREEN ONION WAFFLES

I know what you're thinking. Matt, cauliflower doesn't belong in a chicken chapter. And normally I would agree with you. But as a staunch meat eater, I assure you, cauliflower can hold its own. The trick to making it work is to treat it just like you would chicken: soak in buttermilk, dredge in flour, fry, add sauce. With all these tricks, cauliflower makes for a great vegetarian version of what is normally a meat-heavy dish. (I can't believe I just said that.)

SERVES 4

IT'S CAULIFLOWER'S TIME TO SHINE . . . AND FRY

Bring a large pot of water to a boil. Add the cauliflower wedges and cook for 5 minutes. Drain and immediately place in an ice bath to stop cooking. Drain again, place the cauliflower in a large bowl, and cover with the buttermilk. Cover and refrigerate for at least 30 minutes.

Fill a deep-fryer or large pot with canola oil and heat to 350°F (180°C). See page 76 for instructions and tips on how to best fry in a large pot.

Place the flour in another large bowl. Remove the cauliflower from the buttermilk one piece at a time and dredge it in the flour. Ensure that all the nooks and crannies are covered with flour. Place the cauliflower in the fryer or pot and cook for 6 minutes, or until tender on the inside and super crispy on the outside. Drain the cauliflower on paper towels and season with salt.

NO TWO WAFFLES ARE ALIKE

Preheat a non-stick waffle iron. In a large bowl whisk together the flour, baking powder, sugar, ginger, and salt. In a separate bowl whisk together the milk and eggs. Add the wet ingredients to the dry ingredients and stir until the batter is smooth. Fold in the chili pepper and green onion. Grease the waffle iron, ladle in the batter, and cook for 5 minutes, or until the waffles are golden brown. Repeat to make 4 waffles.

In a small bowl stir together the plum sauce and sambal oelek.

To assemble, place a Green Onion Waffle on each plate and top each with one wedge of Fried Cauliflower. Drizzle with Chili Plum Sauce and garnish with sliced green onion.

Fried Cauliflower

1 head cauliflower, cut into quarters

3 cups (750 mL) buttermilk

16 cups (4 L) canola oil

2 cups (500 mL) all-purpose flour

Salt

Green Onion Waffles

4 cups (1 L) all-purpose flour

2 tablespoons + 2 teaspoons (40 mL) baking powder

2 teaspoons (10 mL) white sugar

1 teaspoon (5 mL) ground ginger

1 teaspoon (5 mL) salt

3½ cups (875 mL) 2% or whole milk

4 large eggs

2 Thai red chili peppers, diced with seeds

½ cup (125 mL) finely chopped green onion

Chili Plum Sauce

½ cup (125 mL) plum sauce

½ cup (125 mL) sambal oelek

For Garnish

¼ cup (60 mL) thinly sliced green onion

Anatomy of Bacon

It's like an alarm clock you can eat

CANADIAN BACON
A.K.A. PEAMEAL BACON

In my opinion, the bacon
champion. Often served on a
bun, this beauty comes from the
loin of the pig. It's brined with
curing salt for roughly six days,
rolled in cornmeal, and sliced by
hand. Grill, top with cheese, and
politely enjoy.

HAM

Sweet, honey-suckling, smoky ham. Often taken from the rear or hind of the pig. It's brined first, then smoked, then shaved, then grilled, then eaten . . . with eggs.

BACON

Otherwise known as pig candy. The perfect ratio of meat and fat and salt. One third of the BLT, and to be honest, the most important third, at that. This cut comes from the belly of the pig and is brined, smoked, sliced, and grilled until crispy (not burnt).

Family-Style
Brunch

BRUNCH IS A culture, a routine, and a feeling. While the food is the vehicle, it's the act of eating together that really is what brunch is all about. I love digging into my own plate of chicken and waffles, but sometimes doing brunch family style is the way to go. (And that way I can eat half of Ky's pancakes and not feel bad about it.) In this chapter I've included some of the most sharable brunch recipes. Quite often I layer textures and flavours that come together in one pot or cast-iron skillet, like my Shakshuka (page 102), where everyone eating needs to rip some rustic bread and just start dipping. The Shrimp and Grit Quiche with Polenta Crust (page 113) bakes up crispy and cheesy and is perfect served family style on a big harvest table. These are warm, comforting dishes that not only make you feel good when you eat them, but by virtue of sharing them with others, allow you to connect with your friends and family and become fully immersed in the ritual of brunch.

SHAKSHUKA

When we opened our restaurant Lisa Marie, it's safe to say that we put a lot of stock in meat-heavy options and not much in the way of vegetables. Yes, meat is beautiful, but so are tasty vegetarian dishes. Now we have plenty of hearty veggie options available on both the brunch and dinner menus. The one that started it all was this dish—Middle Eastern spiced tomatoes with roasted eggplant and zucchini, baked eggs, and bread. It's smoky, spicy, and meaty (despite its lack of meat), and in my opinion it's the perfect brunch dish.

SERVES 2 TO 4

Roasted Vegetables

2 cups (500 mL) cubed eggplant

2 cups (500 mL) zucchini cut into half moons

2 cups (500 mL) thickly sliced sweet yellow pepper

2 tablespoons (30 mL) canola oil

1 teaspoon (5 mL) salt

Spicy Lentil Sauce

1 tablespoon (15 mL) canola oil

1 cup (250 mL) minced yellow onion

¼ cup (60 mL) minced garlic (about 6 cloves)

1 teaspoon (5 mL) salt

½ teaspoon (2 mL) black pepper

½ teaspoon (2 mL) ground cumin

½ teaspoon (2 mL) chili powder

½ teaspoon (2 mL) turmeric

½ teaspoon (2 mL) chili flakes

½ teaspoon (2 mL) garlic powder

1 can (28 ounces/796 mL) diced tomatoes

½ cup (125 mL) canned lentils, drained and rinsed

¾ cup (175 mL) water

1 tablespoon (15 mL) unsalted butter

For Serving

4 large eggs

2 tablespoons (30 mL) crumbled feta cheese

Fresh basil leaves, for garnish

Baguette loaf, sliced

ROAST THEM VEG

Preheat the oven to 400°F (200°C) and line a baking sheet with parchment paper. In a large bowl, toss the eggplant, zucchini, and yellow pepper with the oil and salt. Spread out on the baking sheet. Roast the vegetables for 12 minutes, or until they start to brown and soften but still have some bite to them.

SPICE HIT (ADJUST AS YOU WISH)

To make the Spicy Lentil Sauce, heat the oil in a large ovenproof frying pan over medium-high heat. Add the onion and garlic and sauté for 5 minutes. Add the salt, pepper, cumin, chili powder, turmeric, chili flakes, and garlic powder; mix thoroughly. Add the tomatoes and stir well. Turn the heat down to medium-low and allow the sauce to simmer for 15 minutes. Stir in the lentils, water, and butter and continue to simmer for 15 minutes more. Add the roasted vegetables and stir to combine.

BUBBLE, BUBBLE, BAKE, AND CRUMBLE

Set the oven to broil and make sure your oven rack is near the middle slot. Use the back of a large spoon to make 4 evenly spaced divots in the Spicy Lentil Sauce. Crack the eggs into the divots and transfer the pan to the oven to bake for 7 minutes, or until the egg whites are fully cooked.

Remove the pan from the oven and garnish with the crumbled feta and fresh basil leaves. Serve the Shakshuka family style with slices of fresh baguette.

SAUSAGE BREAKFAST BAKE WITH BISCUIT CRUST

Ky is the mastermind behind this biscuit bake. The first time she made it, I honestly had no idea what to expect, envisioning a bunch of baked biscuits. I was so wrong. It was meaty, salty, cheesy, and perfectly baked. My shock was quickly washed away by intense flavour, and next thing you know I devoured the entire pan and an obsession was born. This breakfast bake has everything that a family-style brunch dish should include: a flaky, biscuity crust; warm oozing fillings of sausage, leeks, and butter (sooooo much butter); and of all things . . . canned mushroom soup.

SERVES 4 TO 6

BISCUIT FOR THE BAKE

In a large bowl whisk together the flour, sugar, baking powder, and salt. Use the large holes of a cheese grater to grate the frozen butter into the dry ingredients. Crumble the grated butter and flour together with your hands until the mixture resembles pea-size crumbles. Fold in the sweet corn. Add the milk and stir everything together to form a dough. Wrap the dough in plastic wrap and chill in the refrigerator until you're ready to use.

SAUSAGE AND LEEKS AND CHEESE, OH MY . . .

Remove the sausages from their casings. Melt the butter in a large frying pan over medium-low heat. Add the leeks and cook for 5 minutes, stirring frequently. Increase the heat to medium and add the sausage meat. Break the sausage apart with the back of a spoon and cook for 15 minutes, or until golden brown. Add the parsley and pepper and stir to combine. Turn the heat down to low and stir in the mushroom soup and heavy cream. Remove from the heat and set aside.

Heat the canola oil in a large frying pan over medium heat. Add the spinach and cook, stirring frequently, for 2 to 3 minutes, or until wilted. Remove from the heat and set aside. Crack the eggs into a bowl and whisk until smooth.

NOW WE BAKE

Preheat the oven to 375°F (190°C) and lightly butter a 15- x 18-inch (1.8 L) casserole dish. On a lightly floured surface, roll out the chilled Biscuit Dough into a 16- x 19-inch (40 x 48 cm) rectangle. Spread the sausage mixture in the casserole dish, top evenly with the sautéed spinach, and evenly pour over the whisked eggs. Lay the Biscuit Dough over top, trim any overhanging dough, and sprinkle with the cheddar. Bake for 35 minutes, or until the crust is golden brown, the filling is bubbling with excitement, and the cheese has melted onto the crust, giving it a bit of a crispy top. Let cool for about 10 minutes before serving family style.

Biscuit Dough

2½ cups (625 mL) all-purpose flour

1 tablespoon (15 mL) sugar

1 tablespoon (15 mL) baking powder

1 teaspoon (5 mL) salt

5 tablespoons (75 mL) unsalted butter, frozen

1 can (12 ounces/341 mL) whole kernel sweet corn, drained

1 cup (250 mL) 2% or whole milk

Sausage Filling

8 mild Italian sausages

1 tablespoon (15 mL) unsalted butter

2 cups (500 mL) sliced leeks (white and pale green parts only)

½ teaspoon (2 mL) dried parsley

½ teaspoon (2 mL) black pepper

1 can (10 ounces/284 mL) cream of mushroom soup

1 cup (250 mL) heavy (35%) cream

For Serving

2 tablespoons (30 mL) canola oil

6 ounces (300 g) fresh spinach (about 2 cups/500 mL)

8 large eggs

1 cup (250 mL) grated cheddar cheese

ROASTED EGGPLANT WITH BAKED EGGS

Sometimes—and I do stress the word *sometimes*—I'm in the mood for something a little less over the top when it comes to brunch. I've always loved cooking with eggplant. It acts like a sponge, absorbing all the wonderful flavours and spices that are used alongside it. Its texture can transform in so many ways, from crispy to soft and everything in between. Here, the firm and crispy eggplant skin holds a delicious stuffing, which includes the tender eggplant flesh. This dish is a great choice for a healthier baked brunch option that looks as amazing as it tastes.

SERVES 4

2 large eggplants
2 tablespoons (30 mL) canola oil, divided
1 cup (250 mL) sliced yellow onion
¼ cup (60 mL) minced garlic
1 cup (250 mL) canned chickpeas,
    drained and rinsed
3 tablespoons (45 mL) tahini, divided
Juice of 1 lemon
1 teaspoon (5 mL) onion powder
1 teaspoon (5 mL) curry powder
½ teaspoon (2 mL) salt
¾ cup (175 mL) chopped fresh parsley,
    divided
4 large eggs
1 teaspoon (5 mL) olive oil
2 large pitas, toasted
¼ cup (60 mL) pomegranate seeds
¼ cup (60 mL) crumbled feta cheese

BUTCHER YOUR EGGPLANT

Preheat the oven to 425°F (220°C) and line a baking sheet with parchment paper. Slice the eggplants in half lengthwise and score the flesh with multiple Xs. Place the eggplant halves cut side up on the prepared baking sheet, season with salt, and drizzle with 1 tablespoon (15 mL) canola oil. Roast the eggplants for 40 minutes, or until the skin is crisp and the flesh is soft and easily scoopable. Remove the eggplants from the oven and allow to cool for 5 minutes. (Keep the oven set to 425°F/220°C.) Using a large spoon, and being careful not to break the skins, scoop the eggplant flesh into a bowl. Leave the skins on the baking sheet and set the flesh aside.

In a large frying pan, heat the remaining 1 tablespoon (15 mL) canola oil over medium-high heat. Add the onion, garlic, and chickpeas. Sauté for 5 minutes, or until the onions become translucent. Turn the heat down to low and add 2 tablespoons (30 mL) tahini, the lemon juice, onion powder, curry powder, and salt; stir well to combine. Add ½ cup (125 mL) parsley and the reserved eggplant flesh and mix well. Remove from the heat.

START SCOOPING

Spoon the eggplant and chickpea mixture into the eggplant skins. Use the back of a large spoon to make a divot in each eggplant half. Crack the eggs into the divots. Transfer the baking sheet to the oven and bake for 6 minutes for very runny yolks or as much as 15 minutes if you like your eggs baked completely through.

DIG IN

In a small bowl stir together the olive oil and the remaining 1 tablespoon (15 mL) tahini. Serve the Roasted Eggplant with Baked Eggs on a large platter, with toasted pitas on the side. Garnish the eggplant with the tahini drizzle, pomegranate seeds, feta, and the remaining ¼ cup (60 mL) parsley.

BRUNCH OYSTERS ROCKEFELLER

Ky and I have what some people might call an "oyster problem." We go to town when it comes to oysters. Topped with lemon or horseradish or hot sauce or a simple onion mignonette; West coast, East Coast; large, small—we love them all. In all honesty, my preference is always to eat oysters raw and simply prepared. The only exception to that rule is oysters Rockefeller. The saltiness of the bacon, the intensity of the garlic, and the crustiness of the panko breadcrumbs completely transform the simple shellfish. My brunch interpretation of this classic goes a little further, revamping some of its elements to complement its newly crowned brunch identity. This recipe calls for 6 oysters, but if you're like me, you're going to want to double (or dare I say quadruple) these quantities for sharing with a group.

SERVES 2

GOODBYE, BACON. HELLO, PROSCIUTTO
Heat a medium frying pan over high heat. Place the prosciutto in the pan and cook for about 1 minute on each side to crisp it up. Slice the crispy prosciutto into ⅛-inch (3 mm) strips. In a food processor combine the crispy prosciutto strips, parsley, arugula, Parmesan, garlic, shallot, olive oil, hot sauce, and lemon juice. Pulse until you are left with a brightly coloured herb paste.

SHUCK OFF
Preheat the oven to 450°F (230°C). To shuck the oysters, place an oyster rounded side down on a clean dishtowel, fold the towel over it so only the hinge is exposed, and use one hand to hold the oyster in place. Insert the tip of a shucking knife into the hinge. Use the towel to apply pressure on the oyster as you wiggle the knife back and forth to pop off the flat top shell. Carefully slide the shucking knife between the oyster and the top shell to sever the muscle and ensure the oyster is free.

FILL, BAKE, EAT, REPEAT
Arrange the oysters in a baking dish. Place a heaping teaspoon (6 mL) of herb paste on each oyster and sprinkle each with the breadcrumbs. Bake the oysters for 10 to 12 minutes, or until the breadcrumbs are crispy and the herb paste is bubbling.

While the oysters are baking, bring a small pot of water to a boil and add the vinegar. Crack the quail eggs into the water and poach for 30 to 45 seconds. Using a slotted spoon, scoop the poached quail eggs from the water and place them in a bowl of room-temperature water.

To serve, top each baked oyster with a poached quail egg. Sprinkle with chives and season with salt and pepper.

3 thin slices prosciutto
½ cup (125 mL) parsley leaves
¼ cup (60 mL) arugula
¼ cup (60 mL) freshly grated Parmesan cheese
1 clove garlic, peeled
1 shallot, peeled
3 tablespoons (45 mL) olive oil
1 teaspoon (5 mL) hot sauce
Juice of ½ lemon
6 Malpeque or other large oysters
2 tablespoons (30 mL) panko breadcrumbs
½ cup (125 mL) white vinegar
6 quail eggs
1 tablespoon (15 mL) chopped fresh chives
Salt and black pepper

SPAGHETTI BREAKFAST PIZZA A.K.A. THE FRIPASTZA

Both Ky and I spent a lot of time as kids with our Italian grandparents. For the most part this is where we learned to love and cook food. My nonno was a firm believer that no food ever went to waste. Sometimes we had a little bit of leftover spaghetti from the day before—not enough to make a full plate of pasta but enough to use for something else. He would chop up some tomatoes or leftover sausage and toss it in a bowl with the pasta and a couple of eggs, mix it around, and fry it. The result was an amazingly crispy creation that was part frittata, part pasta. My version is a little different, as the crispy spaghetti is cooked separately, becoming almost like a pizza crust to be topped with sauce and eggs. There's something about biting into that first piece of crunchy pasta that reminds me of all the mornings I spent with my nonno having breakfast with coffee and orange wedges.

SERVES 4

Baked Pasta Frittata

7 ounces (200 g) dried spaghetti (or about 1 cup/250 mL cooked spaghetti)

2 teaspoons (10 mL) olive oil, divided

½ teaspoon (2 mL) salt

2 large eggs

Pizza Sauce

2 tablespoons (30 mL) canola oil

1 cup (250 mL) diced yellow onion

¼ cup (60 mL) minced garlic

1 can (14 ounces/398 mL) crushed tomatoes

½ teaspoon (2 mL) dried oregano

½ teaspoon (2 mL) dried parsley

½ teaspoon (2 mL) salt

For Serving

4 ounces (115 g) fresh bocconcini cheese, sliced

2 tablespoons (30 mL) canola oil

4 large eggs

2 tablespoons (30 mL) freshly grated Parmesan cheese, for garnish

Fresh basil leaves, for garnish

1 tablespoon (15 mL) olive oil, for garnish

IF YOU DON'T HAVE LEFTOVER PASTA . . . MAKE SOME!

Bring a large pot of salted water to a boil over high heat. Add the spaghetti and cook until al dente, 6 to 8 minutes depending on the brand of pasta. (When in doubt, taste!) Drain the cooked spaghetti and transfer to a large bowl. Add 1 teaspoon (5 mL) olive oil and the salt; toss to coat. Set the spaghetti aside to cool. This can be done about an hour in advance or you can use leftover spaghetti.

Preheat the oven to 425°F (220°C) and line a baking sheet with parchment paper. Add 2 eggs to the cooled spaghetti and mix thoroughly. Heat the remaining 1 teaspoon (5 mL) olive oil in a medium ovenproof frying pan over medium-high heat. Scrape the egg-soaked pasta into the pan and spread it out so the bottom of the pan is evenly covered. Turn the heat down to medium and cook for 5 minutes, or until the bottom of the pasta is crispy. Transfer the pan to the oven and bake for 5 minutes. Switch the oven to broil and cook for an additional 3 to 4 minutes, or until the top is golden and crispy. Remove the pan from the oven and tap it gently upside down on the prepared baking sheet to release the Baked Pasta Frittata.

TIME TO SAUCE

In a medium saucepan, heat the canola oil over medium-high heat for about 1 minute. Add the onions and garlic and cook, stirring constantly so they don't burn, for 2 to 3 minutes, or until the onions are soft. Stir in the tomatoes. Turn the heat down to medium-low and stir in the oregano, parsley, and salt. Cook the sauce for about 30 minutes, and stir every so often. If the sauce thickens too much, stir in a little bit of water.

BAKE IT LIKE A PIZZA!

Set the oven to broil. Top the Baked Pasta Frittata with the Pizza Sauce and sliced bocconcini. Broil for 5 minutes, or until the cheese begins to melt.

TOP IT WITH SOME EGGS

While the pizza is broiling, cook your eggs. In a medium frying pan heat the canola oil over medium-high heat. Crack the eggs into the pan and turn the heat down to medium. Cook the eggs sunny side up for about 5 minutes. Remove the Spaghetti Breakfast Pizza from the oven, sprinkle with Parmesan and basil leaves, drizzle with olive oil, and top with the sunny-side-up eggs.

SHRIMP AND GRIT QUICHE WITH POLENTA CRUST

When it comes to brunch, quiche is a divisive dish for me and Ky. I'm not a fan. I find them a little boring. Ky, however, didn't think we could write a brunch book without at least one quiche recipe, and ultimately I relented. This is one of our mash-up recipes. I love hearty, comforting shrimp and grits, and Ky loves quiche, so we've married the two. Shrimp and grits, prepare to get *quichified*. It actually makes sense when you think about it. Quiche needs cheese, grits have cheese, quiche needs filling, shrimp makes a great filling. Okay, Ky, you win!

===== SERVES 4 TO 6 =====

ALL ABOUT THE SAUCE

Bring the crushed tomatoes to a boil in a small saucepan over medium-high heat. Add the dried oregano and season with salt and pepper. Reduce the heat and simmer the Tomato Sauce for 30 minutes.

WHEN TOMATO SAUCE BECOMES TRINITY SAUCE

Melt ¼ cup (60 mL) butter in a medium saucepan over medium-high heat. Add the onions, garlic, red pepper, and celery and sauté for 5 minutes. Add the salt, pepper, paprika, and chili flakes and stir to combine. Add the remaining ¼ cup (60 mL) butter, turn the heat down to medium, and continue cooking for 5 minutes. Stir in ½ cup (125 mL) Tomato Sauce. Remove the Trinity Sauce from the heat and set aside to cool.

CHEESY, CREAMY, FINE-CUT CORN GRITS

Place a 10- or 12-inch cast-iron skillet in the oven and preheat the oven to 425°F (220°C). In a medium saucepan bring the water to a boil over high heat. Add the cornmeal and salt and stir well. Reduce the heat to medium-low and add the butter, cheddar, and cream. Stir well until all the cheese has melted. Once the mixture has a creamy texture, remove it from the heat. Carefully remove the hot skillet from the oven. Pour the canola oil onto a piece of paper towel and use it to lightly grease the hot pan. Spoon the creamy cornmeal into the skillet and spread it as thinly and evenly as possible on the base, and up the sides of the skillet. Use a fork to poke holes into the base. Bake the crust for 30 minutes, or until golden and crispy.

BAKE IT AND THEY WILL COME

In a large bowl, whisk together the eggs and sour cream. Add three-quarters of the cooled Trinity Sauce and whisk to combine. Pour the egg mixture into the grit crust and bake for 15 minutes.

(continues)

Tomato Sauce

1½ cups (375 mL) canned crushed tomatoes or tomato passata
1 teaspoon (5 mL) dried oregano
Salt and black pepper

Trinity Sauce

½ cup (125 mL) unsalted butter, divided
1½ cups (375 mL) minced Spanish onions
½ cup (125 mL) minced garlic (about 10 cloves)
1½ cups (375 mL) minced sweet red pepper
1 cup (250 mL) minced celery
1 teaspoon (5 mL) salt
½ teaspoon (2 mL) black pepper
½ teaspoon (2 mL) smoked paprika
½ teaspoon (2 mL) chili flakes

Corn Grits Crust

3 cups (750 mL) water
1½ cups (375 mL) cornmeal
1 teaspoon (5 mL) salt
¾ cup (175 mL) unsalted butter
1½ cups (375 mL) grated white cheddar cheese
1 cup (250 mL) heavy (35%) cream
2 tablespoons (30 mL) canola oil

For Serving

10 large eggs
2 tablespoons (30 mL) sour cream
Juice of ½ lemon
12 black tiger shrimp, peeled and deveined
¼ cup (60 mL) chopped fresh parsley, for garnish

FINAL LAYER OF AWESOMENESS

Bring a small saucepan of water to a simmer and add the lemon juice. Add the shrimp and poach for 1 to 2 minutes, or until they are pink. Drain and rinse with cold water to stop cooking.

Remove the hot skillet from the oven and arrange the poached shrimp on top of the partially cooked quiche. Return the skillet to the oven and cook for another 10 minutes, or until a skewer inserted into the thickest part of the quiche comes out clean.

Garnish the quiche with the remaining Trinity Sauce and chopped parsley. Serve family style.

DR PEPPER AND BLUEBERRY HAND PIES

I've always preferred pie to cake. I love the warmth of the first bite, breaking the flaky crust and experiencing the fruity filling's burst of flavour. I think pies better balance the sweet with the tart, as opposed to cake, which is generally all sweet. This recipe is my take on a childhood favourite that rhymes with "Top Parts" . . . catch my drift? These hand-held pies play around with sweet and tart notes in the jam. Using pop in the filling might seem unconventional, but it's a no-brainer to me: the blueberries are cooked down with Dr Pepper, which provides sweetness as well as cherry flavour. I suggest doing the same thing with cranberry sauce during the holidays.

======================= MAKES 8 OR 9 PIES =======================

POP GOES THE TART

Heat the Dr Pepper in a small saucepan over medium-high heat. Add the blueberries, brown sugar, cinnamon, and lemon zest. Stir well to dissolve the sugar, and cook, stirring frequently, for 20 minutes, or until the sauce has reduced to a jammy consistency and the berries are soft and tender. Pour ¼ cup (60 mL) of the jam into a small bowl and set aside. Return the saucepan to the heat and cook for another 10 minutes. Allow the jam to come to room temperature, transfer to a bowl, and refrigerate until ready to use.

THE *MOIST* IMPORTANT PART

In a medium bowl whisk together the flour and salt. Cut the frozen shortening and butter into ¼-inch (5 mm) cubes and add them to the bowl. Using a pastry cutter or two forks, work the shortening and butter into the flour until the mixture resembles pea-size crumbles.

Add the ice cubes to ½ cup (125 mL) water and give it a good stir. Remove the ice and add the chilled water to the dough 1 tablespoon (15 mL) at a time while stirring with a rubber spatula. The dough will start to clump together but will not be too sticky. Do not add more water than the recipe calls for! With your hands, squeeze the dough to ensure all the flour is worked into the dough. Transfer the dough to a floured work surface and divide it in half. Shape each half into a ball and flatten each into a 1-inch (2.5 cm) thick disc. Wrap each disc in plastic wrap and refrigerate for at least 2 hours.

Line 2 baking sheets with parchment paper. Dust a rolling pin and work surface with flour and roll out one disc of dough into a 12- x 9-inch (30 x 23 cm) rectangle about ⅛ inch (3 mm) thick. Cut out eight or nine 4- x 3-inch (10 x 8 cm) rectangles and place them on a baking sheet. Return to the refrigerator while you repeat this process with the second disc of dough. Keep the pastry in the fridge until you are ready to use it.

Dr Pepper Blueberry Jam

1 cup (250 mL) Dr Pepper
12 ounces (340 g) frozen blueberries
(about 2 cups/500 mL)
¼ cup (60 mL) brown sugar
½ teaspoon (2 mL) cinnamon
Grated zest of 1 lemon

Pie Dough

2½ cups (625 mL) all-purpose flour
1¼ teaspoons (6 mL) salt
¾ cup (175 mL) vegetable shortening,
frozen
5 tablespoons (75 mL) unsalted butter,
frozen
2 ice cubes
½ cup (125 mL) + 2 tablespoons (30 mL)
water, divided
1 egg

Icing

1 cup (250 mL) icing sugar
2 tablespoons (30 mL) heavy (35%)
cream

(continues)

TIME TO BUILD AND BAKE

Preheat the oven to 350°F (180°C). In a small bowl whisk the egg with the remaining 2 tablespoons (30 mL) water. Take the first tray of pastry rectangles out of the refrigerator—these will be the bottoms of your hand pies. Brush the edges of each rectangle with some egg wash, then spoon 1 tablespoon (15 mL) Dr Pepper Blueberry Jam into the centre of each. Remove the second tray of pastry rectangles from the refrigerator and again, brush the edges of each rectangle with egg wash. Place a top on each pie, egg washed side down, and use the tines of a fork to seal the edges. Poke a few slits in the top of each pie—this will allow steam to escape. Now place the pies back in the refrigerator to chill for 20 minutes. Remove the chilled pies from the refrigerator and brush with the remaining egg wash. Bake for 30 minutes, or until they are golden brown, rotating the baking sheet halfway through so the pies bake evenly.

While the pies are baking, make the icing by combining the ¼ cup (60 mL) reserved jam, icing sugar, and cream in a food processor and blending until smooth.

Transfer the pies to a rack and allow to cool for 5 minutes before covering them in the purple icing.

Brunch in Nashville

A FEW YEARS AGO A FRIEND asked me if I had ever been to Nashville. I told him I hadn't, and his response was simple: if you like country music, BBQ, and bourbon, then it is a must. These are all favourites of mine, so Nashville leapt onto my radar. When Ky and I were deciding which cities to visit for *Brunch Life*, it seemed like the perfect opportunity to visit Nashville, adding a little southern country charm to a list otherwise dominated by big cities. And it really is just that: a city of just over one million people that feels more like a big small town.

Both of us were incredibly excited to explore the city, but we quickly learned that the portrait of Nashville that had been presented to us, although accurate, described only one part of the city. For every country music bar on the Broadway strip, there is a legitimate singer-songwriter recording at some of the very best studios in the world. For every BBQ and hot chicken shack, there is a young, ambitious chef bringing new flavours to this city's menus. And for every $2 shot of Tennessee bourbon, there is a sophisticated cocktail or local craft beer. I love Nashville because it has two very distinct faces, each one acknowledging and respecting its counterpart.

First we visited Butcher & Bee, of what I would consider the more up-and-coming Nashville culinary scene. Located in a large, industrial open space, Butcher & Bee focuses on new interpretations of Middle Eastern cuisine. Executive chef and partner Bryan Lee Weever went from cooking in L.A. to heading up this Nashville spot. He carries himself with a West Coast vibe, a quiet yet confident chef who creates food that occupies a culinary space beyond the traditional southern BBQ and hot chicken spots. He knew his restaurant had to appeal to the massive brunch scene in the city, and he serves food that rings true to his concept: shared Israeli Middle Eastern dishes.

Dishes like shakshuka—stewed Mediterranean vegetables with poached eggs and subtle hits of lemon zest and harissa—were a welcome change from the twice-baked mac and cheeses I had been scarfing down on repeat since arriving in Nashville. Octopus poke served on Carolina Gold rice was the most interesting dish that we ate; it was a plate of old and new—contemporary flavours for the Nashville scene, coupled with a more traditional rice, perfectly done. The star dish for us was the Green Eggs and Lamb, a pulled lamb neck Benny with avocado hollandaise sauce served on a classic Nashvillian buttermilk biscuit. Our meal had just enough traditional Nashville subtly mixed with a more creative flavour profile.

Then there's that other side to Nashville, the one that you think of when you talk about Tennessee. We went straight to the source for classic southern food, to The Loveless Cafe. About thirty minutes away from Nashville proper, right off Highway 100, there sits a multifaceted property with a smokehouse, a gift shop, a wedding chapel (of sorts), and of course a country home converted into a diner. Lest we forget the most amazing vintage sign right at the tip of the property that welcomes you with open arms. This is The Loveless Cafe, established in 1951, and serving biscuits and country ham the same way ever since. It's an institution complete with southern charm, red-and-white doily tablecloths, a rooster room (every picture on the wall is a rooster), and hordes of customers who dine there every day to sample classic Nashville dishes.

The aromas are inescapable, and more importantly so is the hospitality. You sit down and *boom*, biscuits hit the table. These cute little pillows are made from a secret family recipe and arrive with three different types of preserves that change weekly. Among ours were peach and raspberry, which were so intense and tart in all the best ways. I'd been told the country ham is the restaurant's calling card, so we ordered that up. I don't regret the decision—it's delicious and tastes like one big piece of peameal bacon. Salty and briny, the country ham comes with red-eye gravy and eggs and is exactly what you should be eating at this country restaurant complete with front porch and screen door. For a lighter option, the one-pound pulled pork omelette topped with homemade hot sauce doesn't feel as heavy as it sounds, mainly because the eggs are so light and fluffy. And to top it all off, we're brought a slice of coconut cream pie. It's one of those desserts that you say you can't eat because you're too full and then you do because it's that good. After these meals, Ky and I undoubtedly understood why brunch was more of an event than a meal in Nashville and definitely recognized why The Loveless Cafe was, is, and probably will always be the benchmark of tradition in this city.

Pancakes, Waffles, French Toast, Oh My!

I CONSIDER MYSELF a fairly nostalgic person. I'm drawn to watching old movies from my childhood (I fan-boy when I watch *The Goonies*) or reliving experiences from my youth like playing with water guns and eating freezies. I'm a thirty-three-year-old child and proud of it. Pancakes also have this nostalgic effect on me. That smell of the batter instantly cooking as it hits the hot buttered griddle. A tall stack with real Canadian maple syrup. The way the syrup pours down the side of the stack. The combination of sweet mixed with fluffy, buttery dough, and then that first bite. It all takes me back to being a kid.

The recipes in this chapter are some of my favourite in the book. I love pushing the boundaries when mixing sweet and savoury, which you'll notice in my Elvis French Toast (page 145) when I stuff classic French toast with peanut butter and top it with candied bacon. Some of these pancakes are decadent, to say the least, and are often layered with something sweet and topped with something indulgent, which you'll find out when you make my S'mores Pancakes (page 133). The waffles completely reinvent a few classic comfort foods, such as my Mac 'n' Cheese Waffles (page 138) and Creamy Mushrooms on Toast Waffles (page 141). How can you not love all these things?! Maybe it's the excitement of my inner child talking, but prepare to indulge. And be sure to wear stretchy pants when devouring these dishes.

OG BUTTERMILK PANCAKES

This chapter is filled with a number of delicious, over-the-top pancake recipes, but before we get into wacky ideas and add-ons, I had to nail the perfect airy pancake with just the right amount of sweetness. I give you the OG Buttermilk Pancake. I played around with the recipe quite a bit until I thought it was exactly the way an OG pancake should look and taste, and now I'm happy with how these stack up . . . (Get it? Stack up, like a pancake stack? Okay, I'll stop now.) From here you can do with them what you like: add chocolate chips, or blueberries, or whatever floats your boat.

SERVES 4

3 cups (750 mL) all-purpose flour

¼ cup (60 mL) white sugar

1 tablespoon (15 mL) baking powder

1½ teaspoons (7 mL) baking soda

¾ teaspoon (4 mL) salt

¼ teaspoon (1 mL) cinnamon

3 cups (750 mL) buttermilk

½ cup (125 mL) whole milk

3 large eggs

5 tablespoons (75 mL) unsalted butter, melted

1 teaspoon (5 mL) pure vanilla extract

1 teaspoon (5 mL) unsalted butter, for the pan

For Serving

Butter

Pure maple syrup

FROM ONE OG TO ANOTHER

In a large bowl whisk together the flour, sugar, baking powder, baking soda, salt, and cinnamon. In a second bowl whisk together the buttermilk, milk, eggs, melted butter, and vanilla. Add the wet ingredients to the dry ingredients and whisk just until you have a smooth, lump-free batter.

Melt 1 teaspoon (5 mL) butter in a large non-stick frying pan over medium-high heat. Using a 1-cup (250 mL) ladle, pour the batter into the hot pan. When the pancake is slightly browned on the bottom and you see small bubbles begin to form on the top, flip it with a large spatula. Cook the pancake until the second side is browned. Repeat with the remaining batter. Stack the finished pancakes on a plate and keep covered with paper towel to retain heat until all the pancakes have been made. Serve with butter and maple syrup.

COCONUT CREAM PANCAKES

Ky was determined to include a coconut pancake in *Brunch Life*. I wasn't complaining—I absolutely love coconut cream pie. I love these pancakes, too, but the best part of this entire process was that I got to try nine different variations to get to this point.

SERVES 4

YOU'LL GO COCONUTS FOR THIS

In a large bowl whisk together the flour, shredded coconut, sugar, baking powder, baking soda, and salt. In a second bowl whisk together the buttermilk, coconut milk, condensed milk, eggs, and melted butter. Add the wet ingredients to the dry ingredients and whisk just until you have a smooth, lump-free batter.

Melt 1 teaspoon (5 mL) butter in a large non-stick frying pan over medium-high heat. Using a 1-cup (250 mL) ladle, pour the batter into the hot pan. When the pancake is slightly browned on the bottom and you see small bubbles begin to form on the top, flip it with a large spatula. Cook the pancake until the second side is browned. Repeat with the remaining batter. Stack the finished pancakes on a plate and keep covered with paper towel to retain heat until all the pancakes have been made.

COLONEL CUSTARD

In a small saucepan, heat the coconut milk to a gentle simmer; keep warm. In a heatproof bowl set over (not in) a pan of gently boiling water, whisk the egg yolks until smooth. Add the sugar and whisk until dissolved. Continue whisking until the custard begins to thicken, about 8 minutes. Slowly pour the hot coconut milk into the custard, whisking constantly. Again, whisk until the custard thickens, a few minutes more. Remove the custard from the heat and gently fold in the shredded coconut.

Pour the cream and icing sugar into a large bowl. Beat the ingredients together for 5 to 6 minutes, or until soft peaks form. Be sure to incorporate lots of air and this process will be quicker than you think!

To assemble, stack the Coconut Pancakes with a dollop of Coconut Custard between each pancake. Top with Whipped Cream and a sprinkling of shredded coconut.

Coconut Pancakes

3 cups (750 mL) all-purpose flour

1½ cups (375 mL) sweetened shredded coconut

¼ cup (60 mL) white sugar

1 tablespoon (15 mL) baking powder

1½ teaspoons (7 mL) baking soda

¾ teaspoon (4 mL) salt

2½ cups (625 mL) buttermilk

2 cups (500 mL) full-fat coconut milk

1 cup (250 mL) condensed milk

3 large eggs

5 tablespoons (75 mL) unsalted butter, melted

1 teaspoon (5 mL) unsalted butter, for the pan

Coconut Custard

¼ cup (60 mL) coconut milk

5 large egg yolks

⅓ cup (75 mL) white sugar

¼ cup (60 mL) sweetened shredded coconut

Whipped Cream

2 cups (500 mL) cold whipping (35%) cream

½ cup (125 mL) icing sugar

For Garnish

Sweetened shredded coconut

DARK CHERRY CHEESECAKE PANCAKES

I haven't always been a fan of cheesecake, but after trying dozens of varieties over the years, my feelings have changed. Originally, all I could taste was that over-processed cheese filling, but then one year my mom started making them from scratch using raspberries and cherries from our family's garden. The punch of tasty fresh fruit cut through the over-saturated cheese filling. Now we are at a point where Ky and I have a hard time saying no to dessert, especially if the words *cheese* or *cake* or *cheesecake* are involved. Pancakes make for an unexpectedly fantastic cheesecake vessel because you can layer all those delicious components. The layers allow for the perfect ratio of cream cheese icing to fruit filling—and of course pancake—in every bite.

SERVES 4

Dark Cherry Sauce
1 cup (250 mL) water, divided
3 cups (750 mL) frozen pitted black
    cherries
¼ cup (60 mL) pure maple syrup
1 tablespoon (15 mL) white sugar
1 tablespoon (15 mL) potato starch

Cream Cheese Icing
1 pound (500 g) cream cheese, at room
    temperature
2 tablespoons (30 mL) 2% or whole milk
1 teaspoon (5 mL) pure vanilla extract
2 cups (500 mL) icing sugar, sifted
6 mint leaves

For Serving
1 batch OG Buttermilk Pancakes
    (page 126)
½ cup (125 mL) graham cracker crumbs
3 tablespoons (45 mL) finely chopped
    fresh mint

SWEET AS A CHERRY
Bring ½ cup (125 mL) water to a boil in a medium saucepan. Add the cherries and cook until they begin to break down, about 15 minutes. Turn the heat down to medium, add another ¼ cup (60 mL) water, and use the back of a wooden spoon to break the cherries down further. Add the maple syrup, sugar, potato starch, and the remaining ¼ cup (60 mL) water and stir to dissolve the sugar and incorporate the potato starch. Turn the heat down to low and simmer until the sauce is reduced by one-quarter, about 10 minutes. Remove from the heat and allow to cool slightly.

IT'S NOT CHEESECAKE UNTIL YOU ADD . . .
In a food processor combine the cream cheese, milk, and vanilla and blend until creamy. Add the icing sugar and blend until smooth. Transfer the Cream Cheese Icing to a bowl and tear the mint leaves over the mixture. Fold the mint into the icing and set it aside.

LAYER AND SPREAD TO CHEESECAKE HEAVEN
To assemble, place a pancake on each plate and top with a layer of Cream Cheese Icing. Dust the Cream Cheese Icing with graham cracker crumbs and top with 1 tablespoon (15 mL) Dark Cherry Sauce. Add another pancake and repeat layering icing, graham cracker crumbs, and sauce. Repeat until you have a stack of 3 pancakes. Garnish with a sprinkle of fresh mint.

S'MORES PANCAKES

One of the few knocks that customers had about the brunch at our restaurant Lisa Marie was that we didn't offer any sweet options. Normally I default to savoury, so the first time I made s'mores pancakes at the restaurant, they were a special I just whipped up on a whim. I posted them on Instagram and the rest was history; they are now a fixture on our menu, and our customers go crazy for them. Nutella-layered chocolate chip pancakes topped with marshmallow fluff and torched marshmallows . . . Needless to say, they were voted the #1 pancake in Toronto in 2016.

SERVES 4

PUT SOME CHOICE CHIPS IN THE OG

Make the OG Buttermilk Pancake batter, folding in the chocolate chips at the end. Cook as directed.

IT'S TIME TO S'MORE

Set the oven to broil and line a baking sheet with parchment paper. On the baking sheet, stack the Chocolate Chip Pancakes 3-high with a layer of chocolate hazelnut spread between each pancake. Top each triple-decker pancake stacks with marshmallow fluff and mini marshmallows. Broil until marshmallows are charred, about 2 minutes. (You can also use a kitchen blowtorch to toast the marshmallows.) Serve the S'mores Pancakes with a sprinkling of graham cracker crumbs.

Chocolate Chip Pancakes

1 batch OG Buttermilk Pancake batter (page 126)

2 cups (500 mL) chocolate chips

For Serving

1½ cups (375 mL) chocolate hazelnut spread

1½ cups (375 mL) marshmallow fluff

1½ cups (375 mL) mini marshmallows

½ cup (125 mL) graham cracker crumbs

BLACKBERRY AND LEMON PANCAKES

It's amazing how a little bit of fresh lemon juice and zest really shines in my OG Buttermilk Pancake batter. Not all brunch dishes should make you want to go back to sleep, and there's something about fresh lemon that lightens up a dish. Layering pancakes not only is a great opportunity to showcase something beautiful but it makes it easier to combine contrasting flavours and colours such as the tartness of lemon and the sweetness of this berry jam. And if jam isn't your jam and you just want lemon pancakes, go for it!

SERVES 4

Blackberry Jam
½ cup (125 mL) water
4 teaspoons (18 mL) white sugar
1 teaspoon (5 mL) pure maple syrup
18 ounces (500 g) blackberries (about
    3½ cups/875 mL)

Lemon Pancakes
1 batch OG Buttermilk Pancake batter
    (page 126)
Grated zest of 3 lemons
Juice of 1½ lemons

For Serving
2 tablespoons (30 mL) icing sugar

WE BE JAMMING
Bring the water to a boil in a medium saucepan. Add the sugar, maple syrup, and blackberries. Stir well to dissolve the sugar, then turn the heat down to medium-low and cook for 10 minutes. The sugars in the jam will thicken as the liquid reduces, leaving you with a gorgeous dark purple berry jam.

BATTER'S UP
Make the OG Buttermilk Pancake batter, adding the lemon juice to the wet ingredients, and folding in the lemon zest at the end. Cook as directed.

TIME TO STACK
To assemble, place 3 Lemon Pancakes on each plate and top with some Blackberry Jam. Sift the icing sugar over the top for a snowy effect.

APPLE PIE WAFFLES

Having created tons of chicken and waffle recipes for *Brunch Life*, I have a newfound appreciation for what a waffle iron can do. As long as it's hot enough, whatever ingredient you put in the iron, a waffle will emerge. What makes these waffles taste like real apple pie is the puff pastry, which is cooked—yes—right in the waffle iron. This waffle has legit pie DNA.

SERVES 4

Allow the puff pastry to come to room temperature. Preheat a non-stick waffle iron.

THE APPLE OF MY PIE

Melt the butter in a large saucepan over medium-high heat. Add the brown sugar, white sugar, nutmeg, cinnamon, lemon juice, and vanilla. Stir well to ensure the sugar has dissolved, then add the apple slices. Turn the heat down to medium-low and cook, stirring occasionally, for 5 to 8 minutes, or until thickened and caramelized.

While the apples are cooking, gently roll out the puff pastry sheets.

Grease the waffle iron. Lay a puff pastry sheet over the waffle iron and spoon one-quarter of the Apple Pie Filling into the centre of the waffle iron. Fold in all four corners of the puff pastry to cover the filling, slightly overlapping them, and close the waffle iron. Cook for 5 minutes, or until golden brown. Repeat with the remaining 3 sheets of puff pastry and the remaining Apple Pie Filling to make 4 waffles.

In a small saucepan over medium heat, stir together the maple syrup and bourbon. Simmer gently, continuing to stir until thickened, about 5 minutes. Remove from the heat and set aside.

WHIP IT REAL GOOD

Pour the cream and icing sugar into a large bowl. Slice your vanilla pod in half lengthwise and scrape the seeds into the cream. Beat the ingredients together for 5 to 6 minutes, or until airy. Be sure to incorporate lots of air and this process will be quicker than you think!

To serve, place an Apple Pie Waffle on each plate and top with Vanilla Whipped Cream and a drizzle of Bourbon Syrup.

4 sheets puff pastry, thawed
  (2 pounds/900 g)

Apple Pie Filling

½ cup (125 mL) unsalted butter

½ cup (125 mL) brown sugar

½ cup (125 mL) white sugar

1 teaspoon (5 mL) freshly grated nutmeg

½ teaspoon (2 mL) cinnamon

Juice of ½ lemon

1 teaspoon (5 mL) pure vanilla extract

8 Gala apples, peeled, cored, and thinly sliced

Bourbon Syrup

1 cup (250 mL) pure maple syrup

¼ cup (60 mL) bourbon

Vanilla Whipped Cream

2 cups (500 mL) cold whipping (35%) cream

½ cup (125 mL) icing sugar

1 vanilla pod

MAC 'N' CHEESE WAFFLES

The trick with this recipe is making sure that the macaroni is coated in more cheese than you think it should need, because it's the crisping of the cheese that helps the waffle keep its shape. Now I know what you're thinking: Matt, you talk about a mac and cheese waffle so casually like everyone's tried this. You're right, it's different, but part of the fun in writing this chapter was taking things I already loved (like mac and cheese) and seeing if the waffle iron could make them better. I wish I had come up with this idea back in university. I could have made a killing out of my dorm room.

SERVES 4

The Mac . . .
1 tablespoon (15 mL) salt
2 cups (500 mL) macaroni
1 teaspoon (5 mL) unsalted butter

. . . and the Cheese
½ cup (125 mL) unsalted butter
¼ cup (60 mL) all-purpose flour
2¼ cups (550 mL) 2% milk
2 cups (500 mL) grated orange cheddar
   cheese
3 tablespoons (45 mL) mascarpone
   cheese
Salt

For Serving
Sriracha hot sauce
2 tablespoons (30 mL) finely chopped
   fresh chives

MAC 'N' CHEESE ON STEROIDS!
Preheat a non-stick waffle iron (I repeat, non-stick!). Fill a large pot with water and bring to a boil over high heat. Add the salt and macaroni and give everything a stir. Cook the pasta for 8 minutes, or until al dente. Drain the pasta and return it to the pot. Stir in the butter to coat the pasta and ensure it does not stick together. Set it aside until you are ready to mix in your cheese sauce.

NEVER USE THAT POWDERED STUFF AGAIN
Melt the butter in a medium saucepan over high heat. Turn the heat down to medium-high and add the flour. Stir well until a paste forms and begins to lightly brown. It is important to cook the flour to ensure your mac 'n' cheese doesn't have a floury taste! Pour the milk into the pan and whisk well. When the sauce starts to simmer and thicken, add the cheddar and mascarpone. Stir well until the cheese has melted, then remove from the heat. Reserve 1 cup (250 mL) of the cheese sauce and pour the rest over the cooked macaroni. Season with salt and stir to combine.

WAFFLES AND CHEESE!
Ladle 1 to 1½ cups (250 to 375 mL) of mac 'n' cheese into the waffle iron to make 2 waffles and cook until the edges are golden and crispy and the waffle doesn't stick, about 6 minutes. If you start to lift the lid and the waffle doesn't cleanly pull away, then you know it's not ready yet. Repeat with the remaining mac 'n' cheese. To serve, top each waffle with a drizzle of the reserved cheese sauce, a drizzle of Sriracha, and a sprinkling of chives.

CREAMY MUSHROOMS ON TOAST WAFFLES

Ky and I were sharing oysters at our favourite Irish bar when we first ordered mushrooms on toast. Turns out it's exactly what it sounds like: mushrooms on toast. But let me tell you, we're now obsessed. It's a great example of how a simple dish executed perfectly can hit the spot. When I was creating this recipe, my initial thought was to make a savoury French toast as the base, but then I was like, whoa, what if we rip the bread apart and—wait for it—throw it in a waffle iron! The little indents in the waffle hold the beautiful wine sauce from the mushrooms, with its creamy pop of Gorgonzola and fresh thyme. And we've put a fried egg on this, so there are even more soaking-up duties for that waffle base.

SERVES 2

SHROOMIES

Melt ¼ cup (60 mL) butter in a medium saucepan over medium-high heat. Add the garlic and lemon juice and sauté for 3 minutes. Add the mushrooms, thyme, salt, pepper, and the remaining ¼ cup (60 mL) butter and stir to mix, allowing the butter to melt. Turn the heat down to medium and stir in the wine and Gorgonzola. Simmer for 5 minutes, or until reduced by a quarter. Remove from the heat and keep warm.

TOAST WAFFLE

Preheat a non-stick waffle iron. In a large bowl combine the rye bread, challah, eggs, milk, and salt. Use your hands to mix the ingredients to form something doughish: moist but not soggy, pliable but still visibly torn-up bread. Ladle half the mixture into the waffle iron and cook for 4 minutes, or until golden brown and no longer moist. If you lift the lid slightly and the waffle starts to break apart, keep baking for another minute or so. Repeat with the remaining mixture to make a second waffle.

IT'S NOT BRUNCH WITHOUT AN EGG

In a small frying pan, heat the canola oil over medium-high heat. Crack the eggs into the pan and turn the heat down to medium. Cook the eggs sunny side up for about 5 minutes.

To assemble, place a Toast Waffle on each plate and top with the Creamy Mushrooms and a sunny-side-up egg. Garnish with fresh thyme.

Creamy Mushrooms

½ cup (125 mL) unsalted butter, divided
1 clove garlic, minced
Juice of ½ lemon
8 ounces (225 g) button mushrooms, sliced in half
1 teaspoon (5 mL) finely chopped fresh thyme
1 teaspoon (5 mL) salt
½ teaspoon (2 mL) black pepper
½ cup (125 mL) red wine (Pinot Noir or Cabernet Sauvignon)
2 tablespoons (30 mL) creamy Gorgonzola cheese

Toast Waffles

2 cups (500 mL) light rye bread torn into ¼-inch (5 mm) pieces
2 cups (500 mL) challah bread torn into ¼-inch (5 mm) pieces
3 large eggs, lightly beaten
¼ cup (60 mL) 2% milk
½ teaspoon (2 mL) salt

For Serving

1 tablespoon (15 mL) canola oil
2 large eggs
Thyme leaves, for garnish

KIELBASA RÖSTI WAFFLES

The rösti potato guy at our local farmers' market inspired this recipe. He is a machine—he waffle-irons grated potatoes and cheese at breakneck pace. As much as I love his version, he piles his toppings on top of the waffle, while I tend to incorporate more of the ingredients into the waffle itself, resulting in a flavour explosion when you break into it with a knife and fork. Ky has gone so far as to tell me this is her favourite recipe in *Brunch Life*, so it's safe to say, this recipe is a must-try.

─────────────────── SERVES 2 ───────────────────

1 large skin-on russet potato, washed and grated

½ pound (225 g) kielbasa, cubed

3 large eggs, lightly beaten

1 cup (250 mL) grated old cheddar cheese

¼ cup (60 mL) diced tomato

¼ cup (60 mL) diced yellow onion

1 teaspoon (5 mL) dried parsley

1 teaspoon (5 mL) salt

½ teaspoon (2 mL) black pepper

¼ teaspoon (1 mL) cayenne pepper

2 tablespoons (30 mL) sour cream

1 tablespoon (15 mL) finely chopped fresh chives

A NICE AND TOASTY RÖSTI

Preheat a non-stick waffle iron. Place the grated potato in a fine-mesh strainer and squeeze out as much water as you can. Leave to drain for 10 minutes.

In a large bowl combine the grated potato, kielbasa, eggs, cheddar, tomato, onion, dried parsley, salt, black pepper, and cayenne pepper. Ladle half of the rösti mixture into the waffle iron and cook for 6 minutes, or until crispy. Repeat with the remaining mixture to make a second waffle.

To serve, top the Kielbasa Rösti Waffles with sour cream and a sprinkle of chives.

ELVIS FRENCH TOAST

Breakfast fit for a king. Wait, not a king—*the* king. Everyone knows that the musical genius Elvis Presley had a pretty weird diet, including bacon, peanut butter, and banana sandwiches. To be honest, if I had a million platinum records, I'd eat whatever the hell I wanted, too. (It's just a shame he died on the toilet. Makes his whole sandwich addiction seem menacing.) But anyways, back to French toast. The layering of this dish just screams decadent: peanut butter sandwiched between fluffy, sweet slices of egg bread and topped with maple-syrup candied bacon and bananas. It'll have you singing thank you, thank you very much.

SERVES 4

BACON MAKES EVERYTHING BETTER

Heat a medium frying pan over high heat and cook the bacon until crispy. Use a slotted spoon to remove the bacon from the pan and place it on paper towels to drain. Drain the fat from the pan, wipe it out with paper towel, and place it over medium heat. Add the bananas and brown sugar and heat, stirring continuously to ensure the sugar does not burn. When the brown sugar has melted, add the bacon bits and maple syrup. Simmer gently until reduced by a quarter. Remove from the heat and keep warm.

In a medium bowl, whisk together the eggs, milk, cinnamon, and vanilla. Heat the butter in a non-stick frying pan over medium heat. One slice at a time, dip the challah bread into the egg mixture and transfer directly to the pan to cook for 2 to 3 minutes on each side, until golden brown. Repeat with the remaining challah, adding more butter to the pan if needed. To keep the finished slices warm, cover with a small clean kitchen towel or pot lid.

THE GRACELAND STACK

To assemble, spread a thin layer of peanut butter on 8 slices of French toast. On each plate, stack 2 peanut-butter-topped slices and top with a third plain slice. Top each Elvis French Toast stack with a generous portion of Bacon Banana Drizzle. Serve with extra maple syrup on the side.

Bacon Banana Drizzle

5 strips bacon, cut into ¼-inch (5 mm) pieces
2 bananas, sliced
2 tablespoons (30 mL) brown sugar
¼ cup (60 mL) pure maple syrup

French Toast

4 large eggs
½ cup (125 mL) 2% or whole milk
½ teaspoon (2 mL) cinnamon
½ teaspoon (2 mL) pure vanilla extract
1 tablespoon (15 mL) unsalted butter (with extra in case you need to frequently butter your pan)
12 slices challah bread

For Serving

½ cup (125 mL) peanut butter
Pure maple syrup

OVERNIGHT CINNAMON BUN FRENCH TOAST

I love cinnamon buns but hate making them. Ky had the genius idea for this hybrid French toast and cinnamon bun dish, which I had a hard time visualizing at first, but it tastes exactly how you would imagine. What makes this easy is that there's no need to make cinnamon bun dough (definitely the part that will most likely get messed up). This version takes a bit of patience while the bread soaks up the egg and cinnamon bun flavours, but once you're past that, you bake it, top with icing, and devour.

SERVES 4

Cinnamon Bun Filling

1 cup (250 mL) unsalted butter, at room temperature
1 cup (250 mL) brown sugar
1 tablespoon (15 mL) pure vanilla extract
1 teaspoon (5 mL) cinnamon

French Toast

10 slices tramezzini bread (or white sandwich bread, crusts removed)
5 large eggs
1 teaspoon (5 mL) cinnamon
1 teaspoon (5 mL) pure vanilla extract

Cinnamon Bun Icing

4 cups (1 L) icing sugar
¼ cup (60 mL) whole milk
½ cup (125 mL) unsalted butter, at room temperature
1 tablespoon (15 mL) heavy (35%) cream
2 teaspoons (10 mL) pure vanilla extract

BUTTER, SUGAR, CINNAMON: THE FINER THINGS IN LIFE
Combine the butter, brown sugar, vanilla, and cinnamon in a food processor and blend until smooth. Spread a thin layer of Cinnamon Bun Filling on each tramezzini bread slice. Carefully roll each slice like a mini jelly roll. Slice each spiral in half crosswise and gently re-form so both ends are circular. (This bread is very soft and is sometimes squished when slicing, so reforming it allows the bread to regain the round shape of a cinnamon bun.)

PATIENCE IS A CINNA-VIRTUE
Butter a 9-inch (23 cm) round cake pan. Crack the eggs into a medium bowl, add the cinnamon and vanilla, and whisk to combine. One or two at a time, roll the bread spirals in the egg mixture to ensure that all sides are soaked. Arrange the egg-soaked bread cut side up in the buttered pan. Ensure the spirals are tightly packed into the pan (it should look like a pan of pre-baked cinnamon buns). Pour any remaining egg mixture over top. Cover with plastic wrap and refrigerate overnight.

Preheat the oven to 350°F (180°C). Bake the Overnight Cinnamon Bun French Toast for 35 minutes, or until golden and the rolls are puffed out like actual cinnamon buns. Allow to cool in the pan for about 5 minutes.

FRENCH TOAST BUNS
While the French toast is baking, make the icing by combining the icing sugar, milk, and butter in a bowl and beat until fluffy. Add the cream and vanilla and beat until the icing is smooth.

Slather the slightly cooled Overnight Cinnamon Bun French Toast with icing. If you're like me, you'll want every inch of those French toast buns covered.

Brunch in Vancouver

KY AND I WERE BOTH BORN and raised in Toronto and love to visit other foodie cities. (I think this book is proof of that.) Before we visited Vancouver, Ky had talked about how, in her mind, it is a perfectly Canadian city. I had no idea what that meant until we arrived in Vancouver. You can climb a mountain, look at the ocean, sip cocktails and B.C. wine, go for a jog, hit some trendy bars, and then have brunch in a bustling downtown early in the morning. It really is a great mix of outdoorsiness, food, and culture.

When you ask locals and frequent travellers where to have brunch in Vancouver, the answer nine times out of ten is Café Medina. Robbie Kane has been the owner of this culinary institution since 2008. After working in the food service industry for many years, he saw an opportunity that had yet to be tapped in to in Vancity: brunch. Prior to Medina, brunch meant either a greasy spoon or a hotel. Today, new brunch spots pop up here and there, but Medina was the one that laid the groundwork and is still the busiest spot. The original location was small and served mainly waffles. They outgrew that space, and in 2014 Robbie moved the restaurant to a more spacious location. The new Medina is a gorgeous space, with great natural light, soaring ceilings, and fantastic energy. Every table is buzzing, plates of food are gorgeous, and everything you eat or drink has a story.

The food at Medina focuses on Middle Eastern and North African flavours, and the dishes are bright, fresh, and colourful. We enjoyed their famous waffles and spreads, a platter of house-smoked and house-cured meats, a rustic and meaty mushroom cassoulet, and my personal favourite, the Harissa "Burger." What I was the most impressed by was the level of aesthetic detail on every plate and in every cocktail or cup of coffee. A chef should make every dish taste sensational, but it's another skill altogether to artfully compose those incredible flavours on a plate.

Now that brunch is a sure thing in Vancouver, Café Medina continues to win awards and accolades for serving the best brunch in the city. Truth be told, Robbie is my hero. Medina is incredibly successful all while serving *only* brunch seven days a week. Much like this book, Medina demonstrates that brunch is so much more than eggs and toast. It's an exciting part of a city's culture, one that allows chefs to get inventive and allows diners see the classics in a whole new light.

Brunch Lite

WHEN IT COMES to brunch, I love to indulge. Cheese, (all the) bacon, a drippy egg, deep-fried anything, a stack of hotcakes with maple syrup, an over-the-top Caesar. You get the picture. One reason brunch is my favourite meal is that nobody judges you for having zero regard for a low-calorie diet. That said, I still very much appreciate a healthier brunch option. Lighter brunch dishes can still be just as fun and tasty. These are for people who love the *idea* of brunch but who don't want to overindulge (which is totally understandable!). Healthy really shouldn't mean boring, which is obvious in my Tuna Poke Bowl (page 162) and Eggs Cilbir (page 157). All these dishes hit you with bright flavours and are hearty enough to keep you going for the rest of the day.

BEET AND ROASTED TOMATO TOAST

I love roasted tomatoes. Slice them, sprinkle with brown sugar, and they caramelize beautifully without getting soggy. This dish would be perfectly delicious with only these roasted tomatoes on toast, but all the other elements just take it to another level. The nuttiness of the tahini and the acidity of the parsley salad perfectly complement the sweet flavours of the roasted tomatoes.

SERVES 4

Roasted Tomato Slices

2 Roma tomatoes, thickly sliced

4 teaspoons (20 mL) brown sugar

¼ teaspoon (1 mL) ground cumin

Beet Tahini

2 medium red beets, scrubbed

3 tablespoons (45 mL) tahini

1 clove garlic, peeled

Juice of 1 lime

½ teaspoon (2 mL) salt

Parsley Salad

1 cup (250 mL) roughly chopped parsley

1 cup (250 mL) finely diced grape
    tomatoes

½ cup (125 mL) finely diced red onion

Juice of 2 limes

½ teaspoon (2 mL) salt

¼ teaspoon (1 mL) black pepper

For Serving

4 slices rye bread

4 poached eggs (see page 50)

1 teaspoon (5 mL) sesame seeds, for
    garnish

HAPPY SLICES OF TOMATO

Preheat the oven to 375°F (190°C) and line a baking sheet with parchment paper. Arrange the tomato slices on the baking sheet and sprinkle with brown sugar and cumin. Roast the tomatoes for 20 minutes, or until they are slightly shrivelled and caramelized.

BEAUTY AND THE BEETS

Place the beets in a saucepan and cover them with cold water. Cover and bring to a boil. Cook for 40 minutes, or until the beets can be easily pierced with a fork. Drain the beets, and when cool enough to handle, peel and cut into chunks. In a food processor combine the beets, tahini, garlic, lime juice, and salt and purée.

TOP 'EM UP

In a medium bowl combine the parsley, grape tomatoes, onion, lime juice, salt, and pepper. Stir until mixed and set aside.

To assemble, toast the rye bread. Place a slice of toast on each plate. Spread the Beet Tahini on the toast, top with a few Roasted Tomato Slices, a poached egg, and 1 tablespoon (15 mL) Parsley Salad. Sprinkle with sesame seeds and enjoy.

EGGS CILBIR

Turkish food is not really top of mind when thinking up brunch ideas. However, sometimes the most unexpected inspirations end up being the best. Ky made this dish for me, and I was blown away. Poached eggs served in yogurt with some pita and a refreshing cucumber salad. It sounds so simple, yet the little hits of acid and spice all come together in a delicious, different dish.

SERVES 4

KOOKY FOR CUCUMBERS
In a small bowl combine the cucumber, red onion, olive oil, vinegar, and harissa; stir well. Season with salt and pepper and set aside.

JUST A BIT OF BUTTER, PROMISE
Melt the butter in a small saucepan over medium heat and bring to a simmer. As the butter simmers, use a ladle to skim off the white froth that forms on the surface. What you are left with is clarified butter. Turn the heat down to medium-low and add the garlic, harissa, and cayenne pepper. Allow everything to simmer for 4 minutes. Pour the seasoned butter through a fine-mesh strainer and collect the clear, red butter in a bowl. Set aside.

In a food processor combine the yogurt, cream cheese, and lemon juice and purée.

Heat the canola oil in a small frying pan over medium-high heat and fry the leeks for 2 to 3 minutes, until crispy.

ALL POACHED UP
To assemble, toast the pitas. Spoon ½ cup (125 mL) of the yogurt mixture onto each of 4 plates and use the back of a large spoon to swirl it around the plate in a clockwise motion. Top each plate with 2 poached eggs, a drizzle of Spicy Clarified Butter, and a sprinkling of fried leeks. Serve the toasted pitas and Cucumber Salad on the side.

Cucumber Salad
1 cup (250 mL) diced cucumber
¼ cup (60 mL) diced red onion
1 tablespoon (15 mL) olive oil
1½ teaspoons (7 mL) white vinegar
¼ teaspoon (1 mL) harissa
Salt and black pepper

Spicy Clarified Butter
1 cup (250 mL) unsalted butter
1 clove garlic, smashed
2 tablespoons (30 mL) harissa
1 tablespoon (15 mL) cayenne pepper

For Serving
1 cup (250 mL) plain Greek yogurt
½ cup (125 mL) cream cheese, at room temperature
Juice of ½ lemon
1 tablespoon (15 mL) canola oil
½ cup (125 mL) sliced leek (white and pale green part only)
4 pitas
8 poached eggs (see page 50)

SMOKED SALMON AND BAGEL PLATTER

Nothing beats a good old-fashioned spread of bagels and smoked salmon. The star here is a beet-cured salmon inspired by Chef Matt Obermoser, my good friend and the head chef at Lisa Marie. The salmon will take you four to five days to cure, so plan accordingly, because this part of the meal can't be missed. What I love about this brunch dish is that you can build your own meal with any or all of its delicious elements. I recommend adding large meaty slices of beefsteak tomatoes, capers, and sliced cucumber to the mix. And then there are the bagels, which I always leave in the hands of the professionals. My favourite are wood-fired Montreal-style bagels, and I'll pick up a dozen from my go-to bagel shop to serve alongside all these wonderful toppings.

===================== SERVES 6 TO 10 =====================

SALMON TIME, OH OH (CUE MC HAMMER)

In a large bowl combine the brown sugar, salt, beet juice, and dill. Stir until it resembles a granulated paste. Rub this paste all over the flesh of the salmon. Place the salmon in a resealable plastic bag, add any leftover cure, and refrigerate for 3 to 4 days. Once the salmon has taken on a dark purple colour, use a paper towel to wipe off the cure. Dry the flesh as best as possible—there should be little to no liquid on the fish. Place the fish skin side down on a baking sheet and refrigerate, uncovered, for one more day. This allows the cured fish to firm up before slicing.

Place the fish skin side down on a cutting board. Using a long, thin sharp knife, slice the salmon diagonally, starting from the meatier end and working towards the tail. Cut right down to the skin but then turn the blade so you do not cut all the way through and the flesh separates from the skin. Cover and refrigerate until you are ready to put the platter together. The cured salmon can be stored in the refrigerator wrapped in plastic wrap for up to 1 week.

CREAM CHEESE IS THE BEEZ NEEZ

Set the oven to broil. Place the garlic on a small baking sheet and roast for 5 minutes. Allow the garlic to cool before peeling. Place peeled roasted garlic, cream cheese, cream, and garlic powder in a food processor and pulse until the mixture is as smooth as possible. Refrigerate until ready to serve.

PICKLED ONIONS, MORE LIKE PICKLED FUNIONS!

Combine the vinegar, salt, and sugar in a wide, shallow dish. Submerge the sliced onion in the vinegar, cover, and allow to sit for at least 15 minutes and no more than an hour. (If it sits too long, the vinegar becomes overwhelming.) Drain the onions and set aside at room temperature until ready to serve.

(continues)

Beet-Cured Salmon

1½ cups (375 mL) brown sugar

1½ cups (375 mL) kosher salt

¾ cup (175 mL) beet juice

½ cup (125 mL) finely chopped fresh dill

1 skin-on salmon fillet (2 pounds/900 g)

Roasted Garlic Cream Cheese

1 head garlic

12 ounces (340 g) cream cheese

2 tablespoons (30 mL) heavy (35%) cream

¼ teaspoon (1 mL) garlic powder

Quick Pickled Onions

¼ cup (60 mL) apple cider vinegar

1 teaspoon (5 mL) salt

Pinch of sugar

1 red onion, thinly sliced

Proper Egg Salad

8 large eggs

¼ cup (60 mL) minced green onion

¼ cup (60 mL) minced shallots

2 tablespoons (30 mL) mayonnaise

½ teaspoon (2 mL) salt

½ teaspoon (2 mL) onion powder

½ teaspoon (2 mL) ground cumin

¼ teaspoon (1 mL) turmeric

¼ teaspoon (1 mL) chili flakes

1 teaspoon (5 mL) minced fresh chives, for garnish

For Serving

6 to 10 bagels

1 tomato, thinly sliced

½ English cucumber, thinly sliced

Capers, for garnish

EGG SALAD FOR THE SOUL

Fill a medium pot with water and lower the eggs in gently. Bring to a boil over high heat and cook for 10 minutes, until hardboiled. Drain the eggs and rinse under cold water. Peel the eggs and give them a rough chop. In a medium bowl combine the chopped eggs, green onion, shallots, mayonnaise, salt, onion powder, cumin, turmeric, and chili flakes. Stir to combine. Sprinkle the egg salad with chives.

To assemble, fan the Beet-Cured Salmon slices on a large platter. Arrange the Roasted Garlic Cream Cheese, Quick Pickled Onions, and Proper Egg Salad on the platter and serve with bagels, tomato, cucumber, and capers on the side.

TUNA POKE BOWL

Poke has become a thing. Like most food trends, when done well, it's actually an amazing dish. Fresh fish, crunchy and tangy vegetables, the perfect amount of citrus, ginger, and sesame. Combine all those flavours with a beautiful egg yolk, and this dish comes alive. If you want to make this even healthier you can substitute whole grain brown rice or multigrain wild rice for the sushi rice. A perfect lighter brunch option!

SERVES 4

Perfect Rice

2 cups (500 mL) sushi rice, such as
    Calrose
2 cups (500 mL) water
¼ cup (60 mL) rice wine vinegar
¼ cup (60 mL) white wine vinegar
2 tablespoons (30 mL) white sugar
1 teaspoon (5 mL) salt

Poke Dressing

½ cup (125 mL) sesame oil
Juice of 3 limes
2 tablespoons (30 mL) rice wine vinegar
1 tablespoon (15 mL) soy sauce
1½ teaspoons (7 mL) grated fresh ginger
1 teaspoon (5 mL) salt
1 teaspoon (5 mL) wasabi paste
1 teaspoon (5 mL) honey
1 tablespoon (15 mL) sesame seeds

The Bowl

1 pound (450 g) sushi-grade ahi tuna
    steaks, cubed
¾ cup (175 mL) shelled edamame
1 pear, diced
4 radishes, thinly sliced
¾ cup (175 mL) diced celery
1 teaspoon (5 mL) canola oil
4 quail eggs
¼ cup (60 mL) sliced green onion
2 large sheets of nori, torn into small
    pieces
1 teaspoon (5 mL) sesame seeds

RICE LINES THE BOWL

Rinse the rice in a strainer and transfer to a large saucepan. Add the water and bring to a boil over high heat. Once boiling, reduce the heat to low, cover, and cook for 10 minutes. Remove the pot from the heat, keeping the lid on. In another saucepan combine the rice wine vinegar, white wine vinegar, sugar, and salt. Simmer over low heat only long enough to dissolve the sugar and salt. Pour the vinegar solution over the cooked rice and fold everything together gently. Cover the pot and set aside to cool for at least 10 minutes.

ALL ABOUT THE TUNA

To make the dressing, in a medium bowl combine the sesame oil, lime juice, rice wine vinegar, soy sauce, ginger, salt, wasabi, honey, and sesame seeds. Stir to combine. Add the tuna to the dressing, stir to coat, and set aside to marinate for 3 minutes. Add the edamame, pear, radish, and celery and stir to coat. Place the bowl in the fridge until you are ready to serve. (This is best enjoyed within that first hour of making it, to avoid the acid in the dressing overcooking the tuna.)

SMALL EGG, BIG POP

Heat the canola oil over medium heat in a small frying pan. Using a serrated knife, cut the top off the quail egg and tip the egg into the oil. Repeat with the remaining eggs. Fry for about 60 seconds. This is quick, so keep your eye on the pan! If the eggs start to bubble, remove the pan from direct heat and the residual heat will continue to cook the eggs.

To assemble, divide the rice among 4 bowls. Top with the tuna and vegetable topping. Top each serving with a fried quail egg, green onion, nori, and sesame seeds.

SPICY BOK CHOY AND MIKI NOODLE SOUP

A few years ago Ky and I took the (business) trip of a lifetime, to Southeast Asia. Singapore, Malaysia, Indonesia, and the Philippines are all very different places with their own food cultures, but one thing we ate in almost every country was soup for breakfast. I lived for it: spicy broth, beautiful noodles, pork belly or seafood, and always a crispy fried egg. Each soup had a perfect balance of vinegar and spice that made me sweat . . . a lot. Totally worth it, and surprisingly made me feel cooler in the scorching temperatures. Functional *and* tasty.

SERVES 4

BUILDING YOUR MASTER STOCK

Heat 2 tablespoons (30 mL) canola oil in a large pot over medium-high heat. Add the celery, onion, garlic, and ginger and sauté for 2 to 3 minutes, stirring constantly. Season the mixture with salt and Thai seasoning and sauté for another 2 minutes. Add the chili pepper, carrots, tomatoes, and lime juice. Continue to cook, stirring continuously, for 2 to 3 minutes, until the tomatoes begin to break down. Add 5 cups (1.25 L) water and bring to a boil. Turn the heat down and simmer for 20 minutes, or until reduced by a quarter. Add the bok choy and the remaining 5 cups (1.25 L) water. Bring everything back up to a simmer and cook for another 10 minutes. Turn the heat off and stir in the cilantro.

JUST LIKE THE REST OF THE BOOK, PUT AN EGG ON IT!

In a medium frying pan, heat the remaining 1 tablespoon (15 mL) canola oil over medium-high heat. Crack the eggs into the oil and turn the heat down to medium. Cook the eggs sunny side up for about 5 minutes.

To serve, divide the miki noodles evenly among 4 bowls. Ladle the hot soup over top. Top each serving with a sunny-side-up egg and garnish with sesame seeds and cilantro leaves.

3 tablespoons (45 mL) canola oil, divided

¾ cup (175 mL) finely diced celery

¾ cup (175 mL) finely diced onion

2 cloves garlic, minced

1 teaspoon (5 mL) grated fresh ginger

2 teaspoons (10 mL) salt

½ teaspoon (2 mL) Thai seasoning (I use Club House brand)

1 Thai red chili pepper, sliced

1 cup (250 mL) thinly sliced carrots

4 Roma tomatoes, diced

Juice of 2 limes

10 cups (2.5 L) water, divided

8 baby bok choy

1 cup (250 mL) cilantro leaves, plus more for garnish

4 large eggs

14 ounces (400 g) precooked miki, udon, or chow mein noodles

2 teaspoons (10 mL) sesame seeds

HEARTY GRANOLA WITH GRILLED PEACHES

Granola is like the older and more mature cousin of cereal. My granola has just a hint of sweet and an earthy texture from the combination of nuts, seeds, oats, and dried fruit. What I love most about this recipe is the peaches: their natural sugars are released when grilled, making this an incredibly flavourful brunch or breakfast dish. And look, no bacon needed!

SERVES 4 TO 6

1¼ cups (300 mL) raw almonds

¾ cup (175 mL) salted roasted cashews

5 cups (1.25 L) large-flake rolled oats

2 cups (500 mL) dried cranberries

1½ cups (375 mL) unsalted shelled pumpkin seeds

2 tablespoons (30 mL) cinnamon

1 teaspoon (5 mL) salt

½ cup (125 mL) brown sugar

½ cup (125 mL) pure maple syrup

½ cup (125 mL) canola oil

2 tablespoons (30 mL) honey

2 peaches, pitted and sliced

4 cups (1 L) plain Greek yogurt

MUST BE NUTS

Roughly chop the almonds and cashews in a food processor. Transfer the chopped nuts to a large bowl and add the oats, dried cranberries, pumpkin seeds, cinnamon, and salt. Toss all the ingredients together.

HIT OF MAPLE

In a small saucepan over medium heat combine the brown sugar and maple syrup. Stir until the sugar has dissolved. Turn the heat down to low and stir in the oil and honey. Set aside 2 tablespoons (30 mL) of the maple sugar syrup for the peaches.

Preheat the oven to 350°F (180°C) and position racks in the upper and lower thirds of the oven. Line 2 baking sheets with parchment paper. Pour the maple sugar syrup over the dry ingredients and toss to coat well. Spread the granola on the prepared baking sheets and bake for 25 minutes, rotating the pans halfway through. Bake until the granola is a rich dark brown.

PEACHING TO THE CONVERTED

In a small bowl toss the peaches with the reserved maple sugar syrup. Heat a grill pan over medium heat. When it is hot, add the peaches and cook for 1 to 2 minutes on each side, until the fruit begins to caramelize.

To serve, divide the Greek yogurt among 4 to 6 bowls. Top each serving with 1 cup (250 mL) granola and a few grilled peach slices. Store the granola in a Mason jar or airtight container on the counter or in the refrigerator for up to 2 weeks.

APPLE CINNAMON CRUNCH CEREAL

My childhood didn't involve much breakfast cereal. My parents forbade me from eating "that sugary crap," as they called it, so I got puffed wheat or I got nothing. It wasn't until years later at university that I started trying the library of cereals available in supermarkets, and even then, I still didn't get what all the fuss was about. And then Ky made me this homemade cereal and I immediately noticed a difference. Cinnamony apples, real sweetness, and the clincher: it didn't get soggy.

SERVES 4 TO 6

APPLESAUCE BOSS

In a medium saucepan bring the water to a simmer over medium heat. Add the sugar and stir until dissolved. Add the apples and simmer for 20 minutes, or until the apples are brown and caramelized. Remove from the heat and allow the apples to cool. Transfer the apples to a food processor and pulse until you are left with a paste.

BAKE FOR CRUNCH

In a large bowl whisk together the flour, brown sugar, white sugar, cinnamon, and baking soda. Pour the dry ingredients into the food processor with the apple paste and pulse to combine. While pulsing, slowly pour in the milk, melted butter, and vegetable oil. Pulse until the dough forms a crumbly ball.

Preheat the oven to 325°F (160°C) and line a baking sheet with parchment paper. Lightly flour a work surface and rolling pin. Remove the dough from the food processor and divide it into 4 equal parts. Roll out each quarter into a large rectangle about ⅛ inch (3 mm) thick. Using a butter knife, cut the dough into ½-inch (5 mm) squares. Arrange the cereal squares on the prepared baking sheet, leaving a tiny bit of space around each square. Bake for 12 minutes, or until lightly toasted and dry. Let the cereal cool to room temperature on the baking sheet, then transfer to a large bowl. Repeat this process with the remaining dough quarters.

REAL SWEET RATHER THAN FAKE SWEET

In a small saucepan, melt the brown sugar with the maple syrup over medium heat. Stir in the cinnamon. Pour the Maple Sugar Coating over the cereal and toss to coat. Spread the cereal back out on 2 parchment-lined baking sheets and allow it to cool. The sugar coating will harden.

This cereal can be stored in an airtight container for up to 5 days. Enjoy with milk.

Apple Cinnamon Crunch

1 cup (250 mL) water
1 cup (250 mL) sugar
4 apples, peeled, cored, and diced
2½ cups (625 mL) all-purpose flour
½ cup (125 mL) brown sugar
⅓ cup (75 mL) white sugar
1 tablespoon (15 mL) cinnamon
2 teaspoons (10 mL) baking soda
½ cup (125 mL) whole milk
⅓ cup (75 mL) unsalted butter, melted
1 tablespoon (15 mL) vegetable oil

Maple Sugar Coating

1 cup (250 mL) brown sugar
½ cup (125 mL) pure maple syrup
1 teaspoon (5 mL) cinnamon

Brunch in New York City

RARELY DO YOU VISIT A CITY that has an actual pulse. New York is just that: alive through and through with millions of people, endless history, unimaginable talent, art, music, and of course, like every other great city, a complete dedication to food. Ky and I are always overwhelmed (in the best way possible) by the culinary offerings spread across the different parts of the city. It's nearly impossible to choose from among all these amazing establishments, and in all honesty, we've never eaten at the same restaurant twice on all our trips to NYC.

When deciding where to brunch in the city, we had to give it some careful thought. For us, brunch is intrinsically community based, and even in New York, where there are so many options, it's clear which places are strictly restaurants and which are part of a community. Enter Sarah Schneider and Demetri Makoulis, owners of the famed restaurant Egg Shop, located in SoHo. Sarah felt there was a gap in the middle ground of wholesome yet sophisticated brunch offerings. Yes, you could get eggs and bagels, but you couldn't do it in an environment that was somewhere you wanted to be (a.k.a. someplace cool). Sarah dreamed of something that was healthy yet indulgent; a place where you could get a messy egg sandwich or a healthy protein bowl and Instagram your surroundings at the same time. So she built it herself.

Whether it was intentional or not, Sarah's fifteen-year fashion career is very much visible in her restaurant. She did not want to open a brunch place that mimicked a diner or truck stop, and she didn't want anything to be yellow. Her simple design and refined colour palette created a brand that is incredibly Instagram worthy. Egg Shop is the perfect relaxed yet hip spot to grab a classic egg sandwich. This playful, modern space is still a place where people can connect with each other and with their food. Egg Shop serves classics, like steak and eggs or fried chicken, but executed in a way you wouldn't associate with a diner. They use the very best grass-fed beef tenderloin steak and organic, naturally raised chicken, and they have made that the standard for everything they serve. Sarah has tailored a spectrum of offerings that speak to the varying types of people that frequent Egg Shop, whether they're annihilating the Eggshop B.E.C. sandwich, with its gooey sharp cheddar and smoky ham, or mindfully indulging in the healthy brunch bowl, which satisfies without the typical brunch heaviness. Sarah really is the food outsider who was inspired to create something that she truly wanted for her city.

From SoHo to the West Village, we headed to Joseph Leonard. Chef Patrick McGrath makes food that he wants to eat at brunch—a formula that has proven successful. While we were there, this cute dining room filled and refilled with hungry brunch-goers. The line was long, but tables were flipping quickly, so no one felt they were waiting forever to eat. In fact, everyone in the room was smiling. Here at Joseph Leonard you can really feel that diners enjoy brunch because it is an opportunity to cut loose and indulge on the weekend. Joseph Leonard's food lies somewhere in between hip NYC pub and classic French bistro. Their fun, playful menu features a wide array of offerings: on the one hand, you can dine on the juiciest double brunch burger ever, or if you prefer, there's a simple and fluffy omelette with whipped goat cheese and ratatouille. There's fresh house-smoked salmon flatbread for the lighter-brunch enthusiast, or chicken and waffles for two, served family style and designed to encourage taking a nap over anything else productive for the day. At Joseph Leonard, brunch is treated as the cornerstone of what you do for the rest of your day, which I love. In a city like New York, it's almost impossible to please everyone, but Joseph Leonard has created a space and a menu for brunch lovers, and no matter who you are, there really is something for everyone to enjoy.

Brunch with a Side of . . .

BRUNCH LIFE IS partly about the amazing, over-the-top brunch dishes that personify this wonderful meal. On most weekends, brunch culture reveals hungry diners craving, if not idolizing, certain dishes, whether it be the most outrageous Benny or the most decadent pancakes. But now it's time to show some love for the unsung hero of brunch—the side dish. Yes, it's true, sometimes they're there simply to fill the plate. But if you're going to put the effort into making these dishes, and give up calorie space to eat them, then they should be able to stand alone! Whether you decide to make one of my chicken and waffle variations (pages 78–95), a delicious egg dish, or that burger you remember that had an egg stuffed into it (page 36), the recipes in this chapter go well with all of them because every brunch needs a side of something awesome. Whether it's Cheese, Chive, and Sriracha Biscuits (page 190), creamy Cheddar Hominy Grits (page 189), or glorious Dijon and Duck Fat Home Fries (page 185), think of each of these as an edible wingman.

ORANGE, GINGER, AND HONEY BACON

Bacon. Bacon. Bacon. Beautiful fatty, smoky, salty, thick-cut bacon. No smell or taste in the world comes close to it. But there are ways to make that wonderful strip even more delicious. This bacon is great as a side, stuffed into a sandwich, or as a topper for a Caesar—the salad or the drink (page 204). Heck, you can even use it as a popcorn topping or sandwich it in your campfire s'mores. Best movie night/camping trip ever. Let's get real: bacon actually goes with everything.

SERVES 4

8 to 10 strips bacon

3 tablespoons (45 mL) honey

2 tablespoons (30 mL) brown sugar

3 tablespoons (45 mL) grated fresh
    ginger

Grated zest of 2 oranges

1 sprig fresh rosemary

Preheat the oven to 375°F (190°C). Line a baking sheet with foil and nestle a wire rack into the baking sheet.

Place the bacon on the rack so the strips aren't touching. Evenly brush the honey over each slice. Generously sprinkle with the brown sugar, ginger, and orange zest. Place the rosemary on the rack to cook with the bacon and bake for 20 minutes, or until crispy and caramelized.

CREAMY SPINACH

Contrary to how I feel about kale, I enjoy a plate of spinach from time to time. I mean, if Popeye loves it, we all should. Now this recipe might make you want to take a nap, versus, I don't know, lift a car, but it's fun nonetheless. This spinach is a great side dish no matter what you serve it with, but it's particularly excellent alongside the Shrimp and Grit Quiche with Polenta Crust (page 113), the Croque Surprise (page 32), or the Lamb Shank Hash (page 11).

SERVES 2 TO 3

Melt the butter in a small frying pan over medium-high heat. Add the garlic, shallots, and salt and sauté until translucent. Remove from the heat.

Bring a pot of water to a boil. Add the spinach and blanch for 1 minute, or until bright green. Drain the spinach in a fine-mesh strainer, pressing down on the greens to ensure all excess water has been removed. Transfer the blanched spinach to a food processor and add the cream and the sautéed garlic and shallots. Pulse 4 times. You want it creamy, but not soupy—somewhere in the middle. Serve immediately.

2 tablespoons (30 mL) unsalted butter
2 cloves garlic, minced
2 shallots, finely diced
1 teaspoon (5 mL) salt
8 ounces (225 g) fresh spinach
¼ cup (60 mL) heavy (35%) cream

SOUTHERN BUTTERED KALE

My mom has been cooking kale for years, and my resistance to it has nothing to do with not wanting to eat my green vegetables; my only real beef with it is that I find it kind of bland. As an Italian Canadian boy I grew up eating rapini and chicory—greens that have a real kick. So when faced with a less exciting vegetable, I say add butter, bacon, and onions. This kale goes amazingly well with Pork Belly and Eggs with Creamed Corn (page 15) or my Hot Chicken and Waffles (page 78).

SERVES 4

8 to 10 strips bacon, cut into 1-inch (2.5 cm) pieces
½ cup (125 mL) unsalted butter
1½ cups (375 mL) diced yellow onions
1 bunch kale, stems removed, roughly chopped
Juice of 1 lemon
½ teaspoon (2 mL) chili flakes
½ teaspoon (2 mL) salt

Heat a small frying pan over high heat and cook the bacon until crispy. Set the pan aside, reserving both the bacon and bacon fat.

Melt the butter in a large, deep saucepan over medium-high heat. Add the onion and sauté for a few minutes, until translucent. Turn the heat down to low and add the kale. Use tongs to stir the kale, ensuring that it absorbs the butter, about 2 minutes, until leaves are tender and the kale is a vibrant dark green.

Add the reserved bacon and bacon fat, lemon juice, chili flakes, and salt. Stir to combine and serve immediately.

DIJON AND DUCK FAT HOME FRIES

A side dish can be just as awesome as the main. And this dish is proof. These home fries are a staple on the Lisa Marie brunch menu. Hot and crunchy potatoes covered in grainy, tangy Dijon mustard and smooth and velvety duck fat—hard to resist, especially when served alongside The Great Canadian Breakfast Sandwich (page 31) or my OG Benny (page 50). Duck fat always gives a dish an added touch of rich flavour above and beyond butter and oils, so I definitely recommend picking up some at a local butcher shop.

SERVES 4

Place the cubed potatoes in a large pot and cover with cold water. Bring to a boil over high heat and cook potatoes until they are fork-tender, about 8 minutes. Drain the potatoes and set aside to cool for about 15 minutes.

In a deep pot over medium-high heat, heat the canola oil to 375°F (190°C). Carefully add the cooled potatoes to the hot oil and fry for 8 minutes, or until crispy.

While the potatoes are frying, in a large bowl stir together the Dijon mustard, grainy Dijon, duck fat, salt, and pepper. Add the crispy fried potatoes and toss to combine. Serve immediately.

2 skin-on russet potatoes, cut into 1-inch cubes

4 cups (1 L) canola oil

3 tablespoons (45 mL) Dijon mustard

3 tablespoons (45 mL) grainy Dijon mustard

2 tablespoons (30 mL) duck fat (or unsalted butter), at room temperature

1 teaspoon (5 mL) salt

1 teaspoon (5 mL) black pepper

GOOD OL' HASH BROWNS

As a kid I always confused hash browns and home fries. I mean, potatoes for breakfast, how different can they be? And then a Scottish-sounding fast-food juggernaut came along and popularized hash browns forever. (I'm not saying I eat McDonald's breakfast. I'm just saying I like the coffee and I've tried some other stuff as well.) The major difference is that one is made from diced potatoes and one from grated. I love serving these in a classic diner-style way, with three sunny-side-up eggs, sausages, and buttered toast, or with any of the classics in *Brunch Life*, like my Mascarpone Soft Scramble (page 16).

SERVES 4

2 skin-on Yukon Gold potatoes, grated
¼ cup (60 mL) sliced green onion
¼ cup (60 mL) minced leek (white and
    pale green part only)
1 egg, lightly beaten
4 teaspoons (18 mL) all-purpose flour
1 teaspoon (5 mL) salt
½ teaspoon (2 mL) black pepper
½ teaspoon (2 mL) dried rosemary
2 tablespoons (30 mL) canola oil

Preheat the oven to 375°F (190°C). Drain the grated potato well in a fine-mesh strainer, pressing down on the potato to ensure all excess water has been removed. You should be left with about 3 cups (750 mL) of grated potato. In a large bowl combine the potato, green onion, leek, egg, flour, salt, pepper, and dried rosemary; mix thoroughly.

Heat the canola oil in a medium ovenproof frying pan over medium-high heat. Add the potato mixture and press down with the back of a spatula. Cook for 4 minutes, or until the bottom is crispy and golden. Transfer the pan to the oven and bake for 10 minutes. Switch the oven to broil and crisp the top of the hash brown, about 2 minutes. Cut into quarters and serve.

CHEDDAR HOMINY GRITS

I've eaten grits prepared in dozens of different ways. Some versions I absolutely love, while others I find bland. Not to sound like a diva, but I rarely find a recipe for grits that I like more than my own. True, these might not be considered classic grits, but I don't care, they're so kickass! They have a bite to them, unlike so many that are almost cooked into mush. The way I cook these grits allows them to absorb all that delicious butter, cream, and cheese. I highly recommend serving these with a sunny-side-up egg on top—which transforms this side into a main just like that—or alongside my Sausage Breakfast Bake with Biscuit Crust (page 105).

SERVES 4

Preheat the oven to 350°F (180°C). In a deep ovenproof pan or Dutch oven combine the grits, vegetable stock, 1 tablespoon (15 mL) butter, bay leaves, 1 teaspoon (5 mL) salt, and ½ teaspoon (2 mL) paprika. Place a piece of parchment paper on the liquid and cover with foil. This will prevent the foil from touching the grits as they cook and double in size. Bake for 1½ hours. If the grits still have too much bite, add a little more liquid (water or stock) and bake a little longer. Once cooked, let the grits rest for 10 minutes to absorb the remaining liquid in the pan. Discard the bay leaves.

Melt the remaining 2 tablespoons (30 mL) butter in a large saucepan over medium-high heat. Add the cooked grits, cheddar, cream, the remaining 1 teaspoon (5 mL) salt, the remaining ½ teaspoon (2 mL) paprika, and the dried parsley. Stir continuously until the cheese has melted and the cream has reduced by half, about 5 minutes. Pour into a side dish and serve next to . . . everything.

1½ cups (375 mL) stone-ground white hominy grits

6 cups (1.5 L) vegetable stock

3 tablespoons (45 mL) unsalted butter, divided

2 bay leaves

2 teaspoons (10 mL) salt, divided

1 teaspoon (5 mL) smoked paprika, divided

1 cup (250 mL) grated white cheddar cheese

1 cup (250 mL) heavy (35%) cream

½ teaspoon (2 mL) dried parsley

CHEESE, CHIVE, AND SRIRACHA BISCUITS

I've eaten more biscuits while writing this book than I have in my entire life: dense and flaky, flavoured or stuffed, baby-size, oversized, covered in cheese and eggs, and just on their own. Biscuits are great served alongside your favourite brunch dish or swapped into most recipes in this book that call for bread, burger buns, or English muffins, whether it's The Great Canadian Breakfast Sandwich (page 31) or my Bacon Explosion Benny (page 59). This recipe can be used countless ways!

SERVES 4 TO 5

2½ cups (625 mL) all-purpose flour

1 tablespoon (15 mL) white sugar

1 tablespoon (15 mL) baking powder

1 teaspoon (5 mL) salt

5 tablespoons (75 mL) unsalted butter, frozen

2½ cups (625 mL) grated Gruyère cheese

¼ cup (60 mL) finely chopped fresh chives

1 cup (250 mL) 2% or whole milk

2 tablespoons (30 mL) Sriracha hot sauce

Preheat the oven to 425°F (220°C) and line a baking sheet with parchment paper. In a large bowl whisk together the flour, sugar, baking powder, and salt. Use the large holes of a cheese grater to grate the frozen butter into the dry ingredients. Crumble the grated butter and flour together with your fingers until the mixture resembles pea-size crumbles. Fold in the cheese and chives. Add the milk and Sriracha and mix to form a dough.

On a lightly floured surface, roll out the dough until it is about 1 inch (2.5 cm) thick. Use a 2- to 3-inch (5 to 8 cm) cookie cutter to cut out 4 or 5 biscuits. Place the biscuits on the prepared baking sheet and bake for 12 minutes, or until golden brown. A toothpick inserted into the centre of a biscuit should come out clean. Allow to cool for 5 minutes before serving.

WHIPPED HONEY AND ROSEMARY BUTTER

Here's one for the books: a side of whipped honey and rosemary butter. Perfect for slathering on biscuits (see page 190) or toast or generally just for cooking any dish that calls for butter. Maybe a small scoop resting atop a hot stack of OG Buttermilk Pancakes (page 126). Heaven.

MAKES 1¾ CUPS (425 ML)

Set the oven to broil. Place the rosemary on a baking sheet and roast for 1 minute to release the aromatics. Place the butter and honey in a food processor and pulse until smooth. Scrape the butter into a bowl. Remove the roasted rosemary leaves from the stems and fold the leaves into the whipped honey butter.

5 sprigs fresh rosemary

1 cup (250 mL) unsalted butter, at room temperature

¾ cup (175 mL) honey

Brunch in Toronto

TORONTO IS OUR HOME, where we own our business and have made so many amazing friends along the way. Our love, respect, and appreciation for brunch all started right in this city. From being on the outside of brunch life looking in, to becoming very much a part of Torontonians' brunch community now, is humbling.

Ky and I don't get the chance to brunch regularly, so when we do, we fully immerse ourselves in the experience. On one such morning, we took the day off work and devoted it to brunch. We headed to Toronto's east end, to an area with plenty of people walking around on that warm October day, but not a neighbourhood with many restaurants. We stumbled on Maha's, an everyday Egyptian brunch spot. Now that's not something you hear too often. We put our names on the wait list, walked around the area, and a couple hours later we were seated. The place was absolutely packed, the kitchen had people on people, and the smells were nothing we'd experienced before.

Owned by Maha Barsoom and her two children, Monika and Mark, this restaurant is steeped in tradition. Back home in Egypt, food was central to everything they did as a family. Naturally, when they relocated to Canada, it only made sense to devote themselves to what they knew best. In 2014, the family embarked on a monumental venture: bringing Egyptian cuisine to Toronto. Maha and Monika work in the kitchen, while Mark is the resident barista of true Egyptian coffees and teas that warm the soul and are skilfully handcrafted with robust flavours and age-old techniques. The concept of Egyptian brunch really can't be found anywhere else in the city, and thus this little spot has lineups around the block and is often frequented by Toronto chefs. There isn't a square inch of the space that doesn't tell their story—a wall closet in the kitchen is adorned with photos of family and gatherings back home in Egypt. Maha's is the epitome of a family restaurant; the love that they share with their customers is palpable.

During our four-hour experience, which included chatting with Maha's entire family, tearing up over hearing how much love, work, and passion has gone into the space, and sharing tea, we also devoured amazing food. Dishes all have balance: eggs are perfectly poached or cooked sunny side up and served with a combination of spreads. Heavily spiced beans and legumes and wonderful flatbreads soak it all up. Vegetables are lightly dressed in lemon juice so the acidity pops through in each bite. Our meal was brought out on platters, and all the elements are meant to be combined, which really is the fun of it. (Definitely don't eat the beans separate from the eggs. You need to mix it all together!) Our eggs were stewed with lentils and yogurt, and parsley salad cleansed our palates before we moved on to the next flavour. The proper chicken shwarma sandwich can't be eaten like a sandwich because it's overflowing with hot-sauced meat and tahini and wears a bun top like a baseball cap. There are crispy bits, tender bits, and fatty bits, and it all works together perfectly. By the end of our brunch, we had almost forgotten we weren't dining in Maha's home, considering she combines incredible food with the wonderful comforting feel of a family meal.

———————————————

It was a lot easier for Ky and me to reflect on our own restaurant, Lisa Marie, after having brunch at Maha's. We could relate to every word of their story. They were a family running a business through their passion. We understood all the trials and heartache and love that they felt when telling their story. It might not be our blood family that surrounds us, but we have made sure since day one that everyone feels included in our brunch life at Lisa Marie. When we first opened back in 2013, brunch was something we knew we wanted to offer, but by no means was it the anchor of what we were trying to create. Three weeks after our first dinner service, we started trying out a brunch menu, to capitalize on the Queen Street West pedestrian traffic on sunny afternoons. It would be a lie to say we hit it out of the park from the get-go. Brunch was a slow build that saw many ups and downs. Some weeks the place would be bustling for hours, and others, not a person would set foot inside until midway through service. As we tweaked the menu, we started to gain regular brunch customers, and before we knew it we had lineups out the door. Eventually on the weekends we were living and breathing brunch culture, creating an experience that this entire book embraces. Lisa Marie is a place for families and friends. We open the doors and people mad-dash for seats. The energy is vibrant, the food is unpretentious, and regulars come back week after week. We've created a community spot.

Our brunch is a beast. A five-hour service that never stops and barely lets me and the kitchen team have enough time to drink our coffee warm. We've got it all, from the Pancake Pork Burgers (double-stacked pork burgers that replace buns with three pancakes) to the Bacon Explosion Benedict (much like the one on page 59) to our version of classic peameal (braised in butter and orange juice and served on a bun with fried green tomatoes and a sunny-side-up egg) to the epic dish that is our S'mores Pancakes (which you can find in *Brunch Life* on page 133). From the bottom of our hearts we want to say thank you in believing in our brunch life at Lisa Marie. Yaaaaaa brunch!

Anatomy of Toast

The many stages of toasted white bread

Barely touched, and therefore not really toast.

Good amount of early browning. Personally how I like my toast.

When you spread butter on toast, it needs to look like this.

Moving up the darkness scale. Not a big fan but people seem to enjoy these for their texture.

Okay, so these are practically burnt. Who are you people that turn that dial all the way to max toasting?! It boggles my mind.

Brunch Drinkies

YES, BRUNCH USUALLY is your first meal of the day. It implies morningish. And while a cup of coffee or a glass of juice is a great way to start the day, so is an Aperol Spritz Mimosa (page 210) or an OG Caesar (page 204)—or even both! I love how fresh and light brunch cocktails are. They don't need to be incredibly boozy or super strong, but rather they're the kind of cocktail that complements a meal, and for me, sipping on one is a favourite part of brunch. A WTF Caesar (page 207) and my Round-Trip Ticket to the Moon (page 211) are some of the most awesome drinks and really are brunch's best friend, confidant, and wingman.

OG CAESAR

Like all the other OG recipes in *Brunch Life*, this is the entry-level straight-up Caesar. For those of you who are more inclined to call it a Bloody Mary, a Caesar is the Canadian version that uses Clamato juice in place of straight-up tomato juice. It's better, trust me. I love all Caesars in all shapes, sizes, and flavours. Crazy over-the-top Caesars are always popular, but tend to be more about the garnish than the actual beverage. The OG Caesar is the cocktail you make when you want to indulge in a classic. Because yes, having a lobster tail or a mini cheeseburger coming out of your drink is fantastic, but if that's the best part of the drink, then we've got problems.

SERVES 1

1 lemon wedge

1 tablespoon (15 mL) Old Bay seasoning

1½ ounces (45 mL) vodka

1¼ cups (300 mL) Clamato (or tomato juice)

2 teaspoons (10 mL) Worcestershire sauce

1 teaspoon (5 mL) horseradish

3 shakes hot sauce, like Tabasco

Juice of ½ lemon

1 celery stalk

ORIGINAL BRUNCH JUICE

Use the lemon wedge to run around the rim of a pint glass. Pour the Old Bay seasoning into a small dish and roll the rim of the glass in the seasoning to coat.

Fill a cocktail shaker halfway with ice and add the vodka, Clamato, Worcestershire sauce, horseradish, hot sauce, and lemon juice. Shake until the exterior is frosty, about 10 solid shakes. Pour the contents of the shaker into the glass and garnish with the celery.

WTF CAESAR

Okay, so I'm a bit of a hypocrite. With the OG Caesar (page 204) I'm telling you how much I love a classic brunch cocktail, and the next the thing you know, we're making the over-the-top version. Truth be told, serving this drink with a small beer chaser is fantastic. A nice lager or a pilsner really does balance the spiciness of the Caesar. The spicy elements in this recipe can be adjusted to your taste, but let's be honest: a Caesar has to have a little kick. Otherwise it's just a clam cocktail . . . blah.

—————————————————— SERVES 1 ——————————————————

IT'S THE DRINK THAT'S A MEAL

Alternately thread the sausage, pickles, and peppers onto a wooden skewer.

Use the lemon wedge to run around the rim of a pint glass. Pour the Old Bay seasoning into a small dish and roll the rim of the glass in the seasoning to coat.

Fill a cocktail shaker halfway with ice and add the tequila, Clamato, pickle brine, pepper brine, Worcestershire sauce, sambal oelek, and mustard. Shake until the exterior is frosty, about 10 solid shakes. Pour the contents of the shaker into the rimmed glass and garnish with the WTF Skewer.

WTF Skewer

3 ounces (85 g) smoked chorizo sausage, cut into 1-inch (2.5 cm) chunks

3 slices bread and butter pickles

3 pickled peperoncini peppers

The Caesar

1 lemon wedge

1 tablespoon (15 mL) Old Bay seasoning

1½ ounces (45 mL) tequila blanco

1 cup (250 mL) Clamato (or tomato juice)

1 ounce (30 mL) bread and butter pickle brine

1 ounce (30 mL) peperoncini brine

2 teaspoons (10 mL) Worcestershire sauce

½ teaspoon (2 mL) sambal oelek

½ teaspoon (2 mL) Dijon mustard

MICHELADA CAESAR

It was at one of my favourite taco spots in Toronto that I first tried a michelada, which is a Caesar made with beer instead of hard liquor. While my WTF Caesar (page 207) tastes great with a beer served on the side, this cocktail has beer mixed right in (a little less booze, a little more thirst quenching!). I find that it's easier to drink, stays colder longer, and the bubbles from the beer add a nice effervescence. This Caesar pairs really well with spicy food—like my Singapore Crab Benny (page 55)—as its refreshing qualities immediately cool down your mouth.

SERVES 1

2 tablespoons (30 mL) salt

1 teaspoon (5 mL) black pepper

Zest of 1 lemon

Juice of ½ lemon, divided

2 medium tiger shrimp, peeled and
    deveined

1 lemon wedge

½ cup (125 mL) Clamato (or tomato juice)

1 tablespoon (15 mL) soy sauce

2 teaspoons (10 mL) Sriracha hot sauce

½ teaspoon (2 mL) horseradish

½ cup (125 mL) light beer

Strip of peel from ⅓ cucumber

BEER MEET CAESAR . . . CAESAR MEET BEER

Stir together the salt, black pepper, and lemon zest in a small dish. Set the rim mixture aside.

Fill a small saucepan three-quarters with water and add ½ teaspoon (2 mL) of the rim mixture and half the lemon juice. Bring to a simmer, add the shrimp, and poach for 1 minute, or until pink. Drain the shrimp.

Use the lemon wedge to run around the rim of a pint glass. Roll the rim of the glass in the rim mixture to coat.

Fill a cocktail shaker halfway with ice and add the Clamato, soy sauce, Sriracha, horseradish, and the remaining half of the lemon juice. Shake until the exterior is frosty, about 10 solid shakes. Pour the contents of the shaker into your rimmed glass, top with the beer, and garnish with the poached shrimp and a cucumber curl.

APEROL SPRITZ MIMOSA

A few years ago I went to Italy and visited a good friend in Venice. Although the city itself wasn't my favourite part of Italy, it did teach me the ways of the Aperol spritz. Three parts: Aperol, sparkling wine, and sparkling soda. In my version, I've swapped the soda for a little fresh citrus juice to create a hybrid mimosa.

SERVES 1

2 ounces (60 mL) Aperol

4 ounces (125 mL) sparkling white wine

4 ounces (125 mL) freshly squeezed
   orange or grapefruit juice

3 cocktail olives

WHEN IN VENICE . . . OR ANYWHERE

Fill a wine glass halfway with ice. Pour the Aperol, sparkling wine, and juice over the ice. Garnish with a skewer of cocktail olives.

ROUND-TRIP TICKET TO THE MOON

Cold brew has exploded on the coffee scene. This brewing technique doesn't use heat or hot water and takes longer, but it produces a far more concentrated product. Let's just say a little cold brew goes a long way when using it to make cocktails. The name of this cocktail is quite fitting, especially because you probably won't blink for a good hour after having it. Cold brew has a way of creeping up on you.

SERVES 1

TO THE MOON, ALICE . . .
Fill a rocks glass with ice. Pour the bourbon, amaro, simple syrup, cold brew, and bitters over the ice and stir. Run the lemon peel around the rim of the glass and place it on top of the ice.

2 ounces (60 mL) bourbon

½ ounce (15 mL) amaro

½ ounce (15 mL) simple syrup

3 ounces (90 mL) cold-brew coffee

3 dashes Angostura bitters

2-inch (5 cm) piece of lemon peel

GINGER BEER MIMOSA WITH ROSEMARY AND ORANGE SYRUP

It would be silly of me to give you a straight-up mimosa recipe. That brunch bevy staple is something I think everyone can handle on their own. This cocktail, however, is something special. It perfectly combines three very distinct flavours: the sharpness of ginger beer, the smokiness of rosemary, and the sweetness of orange syrup.

SERVES 1

GINGER BEER IS SO HOT RIGHT NOW

Set the oven to broil. Drizzle the rosemary sprig with the oil and sprinkle with salt. Place it on a baking sheet and roast for 1 minute, or until the oil is hot and the aromatics of the rosemary have been released. Wait for the rosemary to cool, then remove the leaves and roughly chop.

Peel half of 1 orange and finely dice the rind. Juice both oranges and add the juice to a small saucepan. Bring to a simmer over medium-low heat. Add the diced orange rind, chopped rosemary, grated ginger, and sugar. Stir until the sugar has dissolved, then bring to a boil and remove from the heat. The liquid will have evaporated, leaving a sugary syrup behind. Leave the syrup to cool.

FLUTES MEAN ADULTING

Pour ½ ounce (15 mL) of the Rosemary and Orange Syrup into a champagne flute. Top with Prosecco and ginger beer. Lay the rosemary sprig in your palm and give it a high five to release the natural aromas. Place it in the champagne flute to garnish.

Rosemary and Orange Syrup

1 sprig fresh rosemary
1 teaspoon (5 mL) canola oil
¼ teaspoon (1 mL) salt
2 oranges
1 teaspoon (5 mL) grated fresh ginger
¼ cup (60 mL) white sugar

The Mimosa

4 ounces (125 mL) Prosecco
2 ounces (60 mL) ginger beer
1 sprig fresh rosemary, for garnish

BROWN BULL

It's embarrassing to say, but one of my go-to drinks at university was a brown cow—milk and Kahlua. This version gives the original a little more oomph, hence the "bull." This cocktail is shaken, which makes for a nice frothy drink, and a little bit of tequila gives it a more intense flavour than the original.

SERVES 1

2 ounces (60 mL) coffee-flavoured
   liqueur, such as Kahlua
½ ounce (15 mL) tequila reposado
¾ cup (175 mL) 2% milk
Cinnamon

GRAB LIFE BY THE TEQUILA HORNS
Fill a cocktail shaker halfway with ice and add the coffee liqueur, tequila, and milk. Shake until the exterior is frosty, about 10 solid shakes. Strain the contents of the shaker into a rocks glass and garnish with a pinch of cinnamon.

IRISH NUTELLA HOT CHOCOLATE

Nutella is in my soul. I couldn't even tell you how many Nutella sandwiches I've eaten in my life. Let me tell you how excited I was when I learned you could make hot chocolate with it . . . and then booze it up. You can serve this any time of year, but considering it's served warm, it really is best enjoyed in the colder months. Maybe with a plate of my OG Buttermilk Pancakes (page 126).

SERVES 1

NUUUUTELLA-ELLAAA

Bring the milk to a boil in a small saucepan, but keep your eye on it to make sure it doesn't burn (which can happen easily). Add the chocolate hazelnut spread and stir until melted. Remove from the heat.

Whip the cream with the icing sugar until stiff peaks form.

Pour the Irish cream liqueur into a mug and pour the hot chocolate over it. Top with the whipped cream.

1½ cups (375 mL) 2% milk
3 tablespoons (45 mL) chocolate hazelnut spread, such as Nutella
¾ cup (175 mL) heavy (35%) cream
1 tablespoon (15 mL) icing sugar
2 ounces (60 mL) Irish cream liqueur, such as Baileys

ELVIS MILKSHAKE

The King has been a huge part of our career. Our food truck, Priscilla, and our restaurant, Lisa Marie, are entirely inspired by the Elvis busts that used to frequent our pop-up tables. Here's one more recipe dedicated to the King—just like the Elvis French Toast (page 145), it combines peanut butter, bananas, and candied bacon—but this time in beverage form!

SERVES 2

5 strips bacon, cut into ¼-inch (5 mm) pieces
1 cup (250 mL) cold heavy (35%) cream
¼ cup (60 mL) icing sugar
½ vanilla pod
2 tablespoons (30 mL) peanut butter
1 tablespoon (15 mL) brown sugar
4 cups (1 L) French vanilla ice cream
½ cup (125 mL) 2% milk
1 ripe banana, cut into chunks

BACON, OBVIOUSLY

Heat a frying pan over high heat and cook the bacon bits until crispy. Use a slotted spoon to remove the bacon from the pan and place it on paper towels to drain.

Combine the cream and icing sugar in a large bowl. Slice the vanilla pod in half lengthwise and scrape the seeds into the cream. Beat for 5 to 6 minutes, until the cream forms soft peaks. Be sure to incorporate lots of air and this process will be quicker than you think! Set aside in the fridge until you are ready to use.

In a small saucepan over medium heat, stir the peanut butter and brown sugar until melted into a sweet syrup. Turn the heat up to high and cook, stirring, for only a few minutes—be careful not to burn it. Remove from the heat.

JUICE FIT FOR A KING

In a blender combine the ice cream, milk, and banana and blend for 1 to 2 minutes, until smooth and combined. Add additional milk if necessary to loosen the shake.

SHAKE THEM HIPS

Pour the banana shake into 2 milkshake glasses and top each with a dollop of whipped cream. Drizzle both with the peanut butter syrup and sprinkle with bacon bits. Grab a few milkshake straws and chug like the king!

THANK YOU

WELP, WE DID IT AGAIN! Ate some food, wrote a bit, snapped some photos, and lived to tell the story. Ky and I would like to pause to thank a few people for putting up with our shit for the better part of a year while we kindly asked them to eat as many pancakes as humanly possible.

First, to our families, not only for raising us, but for instilling in us the value of a home-cooked meal and for believing in all of our wild and crazy ideas.

To Penguin Random House, Andrea Magyar, Rachel Brown and Trish Bunnett, who have not only stood in our corner at every stage of this wacky little project, but agreed that yes, eggs are cool enough to get their own cookbook.

To the amazing team at Kin Community and Sundance Filardi at the Spotlight Agency. Thank you for helping Ky and I continue to develop our brand in new ways that far exceed walls and dinner service.

To all the amazing cities we visited, chefs we broke bread with, and brunches we crushed, this book is only possible because we all have the same love and devotion to that meal that isn't quite breakfast or lunch.

To our team at Fidel Gastro's and Lisa Marie, your dedication to your jobs has made our ability to grow the company in new ways possible. A sincere thank you.

To Houston Mausner, you took notes, you organized, you recipe tested, you prop shopped, and, and, and . . . You really can do it all, whilst eating the odd biscuit or cheddar grit here and there. Ky and I are so thankful to call you a friend and colleague.

To all of you who talk brunch, crave brunch, take photos of brunch, share stories of brunch, wait in line for brunch, and eat brunch . . . thank you.

And lastly, I would personally like to thank Kyla Zanardi, my partner and my equal. We stand side-by-side at every new venture, ready to take on the world, and I couldn't think of anyone else I'd rather do it with. If we were 1980s wrestlers, we'd hold the record for longest tag team title reign. If you and I were Jedi, then Order 66 never would have happened. I guess what I'm trying to say is, you are amazing and you push me harder than anyone else ever could. Thank you.

Now let's eat!

INDEX